Faith, Hope and Rice

Faith, Hope and Rice

Private Fred Cox's Account of Captivity and the Death Railway

Ellie Taylor

Pen & Sword
MILITARY

First published in Great Britain in 2015 by
Pen & Sword Military
An imprint of
Pen & Sword Books Ltd
47 Church Street
Barnsley
South Yorkshire
S70 2AS

ISBN 978 1 47385 788 9

A CIP catalogue record for this book is
available from the British Library

Typeset in Palatino by
Replika Press Pvt Ltd, India
Printed and bound in England
By CPI Group (UK) Ltd, Croydon, CR0 4YY

Pen & Sword Books Ltd incorporates the Imprints of Pen & Sword
Aviation, Pen & Sword Family History, Pen & Sword Maritime,
Pen & Sword Military, Pen & Sword Discovery, Pen & Sword
Politics, Pen & Sword Atlas, Pen & Sword Archaeology, Wharncliffe
Local History, Wharncliffe True Crime, Wharncliffe Transport,
Pen & Sword Select, Pen & Sword Military Classics, Leo Cooper,
The Praetorian Press, Claymore Press, Remember When, Seaforth
Publishing and Frontline Publishing

For a complete list of Pen & Sword titles please contact
PEN & SWORD BOOKS LIMITED
47 Church Street, Barnsley, South Yorkshire, S70 2AS, England
E-mail: enquiries@pen-and-sword.co.uk
Website: www.pen-and-sword.co.uk

Contents

Contents

Acknowledgements

I am indebted to all those who so kindly helped me to research my father's time in captivity. My thanks go to Keith Andrews and to Meg Parkes for their help and encouragement in the very early stages of my research, and particularly to Andrew Snow of the Thai-Burma Railway Centre, who so patiently answered my many questions, enabling me to establish a timeline of Dad's movements between various POW camps and so produce this account of his experiences.

List of Illustrations

1. Dad in 1935, aged 19, the year after he enlisted in the East Surrey Regiment.
2. Mum in 1941 during her training at the Royal Naval Hospital, Haslar in Hampshire.
3. Dad on guard duty in Shanghai, 1939, wearing service dress with webbing equipment.
4. Map showing the 250-mile long Death Railway from Ban Pong in Thailand (Siam) to Thanbyuzayat in Burma.
5. PoWs at Changi, Singapore, where most of those taken prisoner at the fall of Singapore in February 1942 were initially held.
6. Dad's Japanese PoW Index Card, which shows that he was transferred to the Thailand PoW Administration and became part of Work Group 2 on the Railway.
7. This photograph, taken just after the war, shows the track near Wang Pho (Wampo). *(By kind permission of the TBRC (Thai-Burma Railway Centre))*
8. Another photo taken just after the war showing the track and a train near Wang Pho. *(By kind permission of the TBRC)*
9. The area around Wang Pho (Wampo) showing the dense terrain through which the railway was built.
10. Wang Pho station, photographed in 2003, close to the camp where Dad was held for over eighteen months.

Foreword

A little boy places poppies on a section of railway track which had been built over seventy years earlier between Thailand and Burma. He is too young to understand the significance of that track, only that he is doing something in memory of his great-grandfather, one of the many thousands of men forced by the Japanese to build it. Between 1942 and 1943, over 60,000 British, Australian, Dutch and American prisoners, together with countless thousands of conscripted native labourers, were put to work by the Japanese on the construction of over 250 miles of track between Ban Pong in Thailand and Thanbyuzayat in Burma, among them, my father, Tony Cox. Though essentially what follows is his story, in some respects it may also be seen as that of the many others who experienced the brutality, malnutrition, deprivation and disease which characterised life on what became known as the Death Railway. Some 12,000 Allied prisoners and an estimated 90,000 native labourers died during the construction of the railway, the purpose of which was to provide a supply line for Japanese troops. Camps were built along the entire length of the railway as work on it progressed, housing thousands of prisoners. Many of them, like Dad, remained at these camps for the duration of the war performing maintenance tasks on the track, and there were many more deaths during this time. My father was one of those fortunate enough to have survived but, sadly, did not live long enough to meet his great-grandchildren. However, because of the notes he made of his experience of captivity shortly after he was repatriated, they will one day have the chance to read his story. It is a story which is told in the hope that the sacrifice and suffering of those who toiled on the Thai-Burma Railway as prisoners of the Japanese will never be forgotten.

Some twenty-five years before the fall of Singapore which saw him taken a prisoner of war, Dad was born into the poverty of a south London tenement block at a time when an earlier war was being fought. He grew up to have no memories of his own father, a sapper in the Royal Engineers, who returned from fighting on the Western Front in 1916 having suffered irreparable damage to his lungs and died before Dad was two years old. The strain of trying to raise five children on her own proved too much for his mother and within a couple of years, shortage of money resulted in Dad and two of his four siblings being placed in the care of a charitable foundation which provided for homeless and destitute children. Thereafter they grew up in a Catholic children's home in Surrey, with few visits from other family and no option but to try to make the best of it. Dad said that whilst he had no particularly fond memories of his time there, it had taught him valuable lessons about communal living and the value of friendship which were to serve him well in years to come. It had also given him the basics of the faith from which he was to draw much needed strength and comfort during his captivity. However grim life in the children's home had been, any negative feelings about it were, no doubt, eclipsed by what followed some years later at the hands of the Japanese. It was also whilst he was there that he acquired the name which he later adopted for most of his adult life, it apparently having been the practice of the home to allocate an alternative name to all of the children who came into its care, many of whom were orphans. Thus, although the explanation behind the choice of name was somewhat vague, he acquired the name Anthony, which, as it happened, he much preferred to the Hugh Frederick his parents had chosen for him.

After leaving the home, Dad worked as a porter until he was old enough to join the Army. Given what had happened to his father, he can have harboured no illusions as to the possible consequences should Britain find herself at war once more, and in 1934 enlisted in the East Surrey Regiment. Officialdom required him to do so using the names which appeared on his birth certificate, and to his pals in the Army he was Private Fred Cox. Following a period spent in England, he served in India and the Sudan and China, and was stationed in Shanghai at the outbreak of the Second World War. He spoke of his pre-war Army life with great pride, and said it had given him opportunities to see the world which he would otherwise never have had. He talked of the friends he had made and one friend in particular, Jim, who had enlisted at the same time and served alongside him throughout their time in the Army. The East Surreys were undergoing combat training in northern Malaya when the Japanese invaded in December 1941. The battalion suffered very heavy casualties, with almost two-thirds of their number killed, and were eventually forced to retreat down the Malayan peninsula to the island of Singapore where, on 15 February 1942, along with some 50,000 others, Dad became a prisoner of the Japanese for the next three and a half years.

When war broke out in 1939, my mother, Joan, had been working as a shorthand typist in South East London but had wanted to do something to support the war effort so she decided to train as a Red Cross nurse. After completing her training in Portsmouth, she was posted to Ceylon as a Mobile VAD in 1942. By the time Dad was admitted to St Peter's Royal Naval Auxiliary Hospital in Colombo in September 1945, shortly after his liberation from a prisoner of war camp in Thailand, Mum had been a nurse there for three years. (Unbeknown to either of my parents at the time, they had actually spent their childhoods living just a few miles apart in Surrey, but they were not destined to meet until they had each travelled halfway around the world.) After something of a whirlwind courtship, they married within weeks of their return to England. Three and half years' captivity had taken its toll on Dad's health and, like his father before him, he was discharged from the Army on the grounds of being 'unable to fulfil army physical requirements'. He subsequently joined the Fire Service, but before long this role also proved to be too physically demanding for him. However, the physical legacy of his years as a prisoner of war was only part of the problem.

In 1945 no-one had heard of post-traumatic stress disorder, and yet there is little doubt that that was what he was suffering from. He and thousands of others returned from the camps scarred not just physically, but also psychologically, and the latter was something they were left to deal with very much on their own. At the time, not talking about deeply emotional issues was considered the norm. Emotions tended to be held in check, and people – least of all, men – were not generally encouraged to pour out their feelings. As a result, many chose never to talk about the things they had experienced. However, Dad soon discovered that not talking about what he had been through didn't prevent it from haunting him at night. As he was to write, some forty-five years later:

Having survived the rigours of Japanese prison camps, I came home at the end of November 1945 and, like everyone else, thought that my war was over – a thing of the past. I got married and tried to put the past behind me, but then the nightmares started. I got to the stage where I was afraid to go to bed and sleep because the same dream was always waiting for me, where I was back on the other side of the world and back in time. At last, in desperation, I saw a doctor about it and he suggested that if I could sit and talk about the whole thing I might be able to get it out of my system and start living a normal life. My wife, who could write shorthand, sat and listened to me talking for most evenings through the winter of 1946, taking down what I said in shorthand and transcribing her notes every now and then so that together we were able to go over the various things I had talked about. Gradually, as the months passed, the nightmares lessened and then, eventually, they disappeared completely.

At some point during the long and painful process of talking about his experiences, the idea that it might be beneficial to share Dad's story with others was born. Many years later Dad told me that, when he had first come home, he had found it extremely difficult trying to explain what he had been through to people who, by and large, seemed disinterested, and that even those who did show interest seemed completely unable to comprehend what he was talking about. He felt that perhaps if others were to read his account of those years of captivity, then possibly they might begin to understand what had been happening on the other side of the world when so much attention had instead been focused on events concerning the war in Europe. With this in mind, the transcribed notes were typed up in the form of a manuscript. I don't doubt that Mum had some input in the content, correcting grammar, for instance, but I'm equally sure that the thoughts and reflections were Dad's alone. Various scraps of paper containing jottings about things which had later come to mind were slotted between the typed pages, evidently for inclusion in a later draft, and the manuscript was given a title: *Faith, Hope and Rice,* the three things which Dad believed had helped him to survive – along with, perhaps, a sprinkling of luck. Explaining what he had meant, he said that he had been sustained firstly, by his faith in the Allied forces to eventually overcome the Japanese as much as his faith in God, the latter having been sorely tested in the face of so much needless death and suffering; secondly, by the hope that there was a future beyond his wretched existence as a prisoner of war, without which he would have found it impossible to maintain the necessary will to live when at times it would have been all too easy to give up as malnutrition and illness took their toll; and thirdly, by the daily rations of rice which, often in the absence of anything else, had kept starvation at bay.

In the event, the idea of inviting others to read his story stayed just that, an idea. Having finally talked away the nightmares, Dad was reluctant to continue to force his mind to dwell on something which it finally seemed prepared to leave. He felt it was more important to simply get on with life now that he had the chance, rather than risk his recovery taking a backward step. The manuscript was packed away in a box and consigned to the attic, where it remained for decades. Mum and Dad got on with their lives, raised two children, and spent over forty, largely happy, years together before, sadly, Mum died in 1989. Only then, shortly after Mum's death, did the manuscript once more see the light of day. As a result of having spent many hours reflecting upon the early days of their relationship back in Ceylon and the events which had preceded their meeting, Dad's mind drifted back to the story he had told so many years earlier – a story she had been so instrumental in helping him come to terms with. Desperately in need of some sort of focus to help him deal with his grief, he began to talk about his time as a prisoner of war and about the idea of trying to have his account of events published. Back in 1946, the events he had spoken of were, of course, very fresh in his mind; he had been freed from captivity less than eighteen months earlier. And now, over forty years later, it was evident that time had done little to dim his memory. It had, however, bequeathed to him the ability to view that part of his life with a degree of detachment which had been beyond him all those years earlier when the memories had been too raw to allow them to be exposed to the surface for too long.

Having read through the manuscript he had dictated back in the winter of 1946, Dad recognised that it needed some work if it was to make sense to others. Though he had, to some extent, observed some sort of chronology as he related his experiences from capture to liberation, this had not been a priority. The priority had been, he later said, 'to get it out of my system'. Not surprisingly, as the memories had tumbled out back in 1946, they hadn't necessarily done so neatly in order; rather, his mind had leapt backwards and forwards as one memory triggered another. At the time he had simply 'talked it out', and Mum had noted it down. The fact that some of it was a little muddled hadn't mattered. However, Dad realised that if his story was to be shared with others, it did matter now; there was a need to restructure some of his account so that it made sense chronologically, to clarify points which he had related more in note form than in narrative and to check details such as dates. This he began to do, also adding a few words here and there as further memories came back to him, and writing a brief postscript. With much work still to do, he approached a publisher and also gave an interview to a local newspaper. Sadly, that was as far as things progressed. Little more than a year after Mum's death, he became seriously ill and, after several months in hospital, died before he could complete what he had begun. It was then that I read the manuscript for the first time and discovered how little I had really known until that time about the appalling way the Japanese treated their prisoners and the often devastating consequences for the long-term health of those who survived. I regretted not having asked more questions when I had the chance, and realised the extent to which Dad had tended to play down the horror of his years of captivity. Perhaps he did so from a sense of self-preservation, not wishing to invite questions which delved too deeply into the past or, perhaps, from a desire to shield those closest to him from the awful, grim reality. Perhaps it was a little of both, but it was possibly also from a sense of misplaced guilt at having survived an experience which claimed the lives of so many others. As Dad had, until his final illness, been so enthusiastic about trying to have his work published, it seemed wrong to allow a project which had clearly meant so much to him to remain unfinished. At that time, however, the idea of picking up where Dad had left off and preparing his story for publication was more than I felt able to cope with; my own grief was too raw, and the task too daunting. So, once again, the manuscript was packed in a box and consigned to another attic.

Now, nearly seventy years after Dad's release from captivity, what follows is his story. Much of it remains completely unchanged from the notes he dictated in 1946. However, in order to give chronological accuracy to remembered events, I have continued the process he began of untangling those parts which were noted down out of sequence, so that this account of his experiences has a more clearly defined beginning, middle and end than was the case in the original manuscript. This has entailed linking various parts together using a few words of my own but, for the sake of continuity, and as this represents only a small part of the overall account, I have written those words in the first person singular, thereby allowing Dad to continue to tell his story, rather than my chipping in to tell parts of it for him. In addition, I have incorporated wherever relevant some additional notes he made in 1990. Dad's recollection of the dates on which some things happened seemed a little shaky at times during his account, so I have done my best to verify the timing of his movements between various prison camps during the three and a half years of his captivity and have made corrections to those dates he gave where necessary. This I have done with the help of those whose knowledge of this field is far greater than mine, together with information gleaned from Dad's army record and other official documentation. His recall of some dates, however, appears to have been remarkably accurate, which leads me to suspect that he, like some others, may have kept a diary of sorts for at least part of the time he was a prisoner of war. If so, this would have been done at some risk, since the keeping of diaries was strictly forbidden, and carried the threat of severe punishment if caught.

Dad gave quite a lot of detail about some things, and rather less about others, but I have deliberately sought not to try to remedy this by adding things which he did not mention himself. I felt that to do so would have been to tamper with his memories; better that they remain incomplete. Therefore, what follows is in no way a comprehensive account of the experience of those three and a half years of captivity but, rather, an account of *his* experience of it. Others will have had similar but individually different experiences. At various stages in the narrative I decided it was beneficial to add a few words of my own in order to clarify certain points which may otherwise have resulted in some confusion for the reader, and where this happens, it is noted. I took the decision not to use the real names of those fellow soldiers Dad mentioned, out of respect for them and their families. However, any Japanese names remain unchanged. Throughout his manuscript, Dad frequently referred to his captors as Japs, rather than Japanese, presumably because that was how he and his comrades referred to them, rather than from any intention to cause offence. I have not altered this as I believe that to do so would also alter the flavour of his account. Finally, I have used the same names for the various camps that Dad used, and written them in the same way he did, as these were the somewhat anglicised names by which the PoWs tended to refer to them, as opposed to the lengthier, authentic Thai names for them. Thus, the camps at Kanchanaburi, Wang Pho, Tha Makhan and Tha Muang are referred to, respectively, as Kanburi, Wampo, Tamarkan and Tamuang. Throughout all of this, my priority has been to retain the integrity of Dad's account of his experiences.

It is to the memory of those who did not survive to tell their own story, that Dad wished to dedicate his own. This then, is his story, told, as far as possible, in his own words.

Ellie Taylor

One's memory can play tricks at times, but there are some things which tuck themselves away so well in the corners of the mind that they cannot be forgotten, no matter how hard one tries or how much time passes. Here is that which my mind refuses to forget.

Tony Cox (1990)

Chapter One

The Nightmare Begins

When I look back on the events of February 1942, it's like remembering the start of a very bad dream. I say 'remembering' but the fact is that it never really goes away. I only have to close my eyes and I'm back there once more, on a hillside in Singapore.

Bukit Timah, Singapore, February 1942. Another night when none of us had slept. Perhaps it was the third such night, or the fourth. I doubt any of us knew for certain, we were so exhausted. Perhaps it's just as well that we didn't know what lay ahead. For the last week or so, day and night had somehow merged into one in the struggle to defend the island against the advancing Japanese. Now they had reached the centre of the town, their tanks and armoured cars moving along the streets. It was plain to everyone that, barring a miracle, we were going to be overrun before very long. There was nowhere to go: the causeway linking Singapore to the mainland was impassable; the only other way to get there was by sea, and the few boats that were left would have been bombed before they were out of sight of the island. The situation had an air of unreality. How could this be happening? This was Singapore, the so-called jewel in the crown of the British Empire, about to fall into the hands of a seemingly unstoppable enemy.

The Japanese had invaded Malaya in December 1941 and we had fought hard to try to hold them back, but it was no good, they just kept on coming; they were a formidable force and our battalion suffered heavy casualties. By the beginning of February, just about every able-bodied man was over on Singapore. Our sick and wounded were being taken away as fast as the few remaining ships could safely leave the island, although for some of them the journey had hardly begun before it was ended by Japanese bombing. We had heard that two of our ships had been sunk. Our spirits had already been getting low but this was devastating news to make them plummet even further. The Japanese hadn't been expected to launch an attack on the island of Singapore from the north, but that is exactly what they did. As they attempted a crossing from the mainland, Australian machine gunners positioned on the north side of the island put up a fierce fight and inflicted heavy casualties, but the Japanese attack was relentless. Before long, despite the efforts of our forces, they crossed to Singapore. All they needed was a foothold, and they got one. They crossed on rafts, on logs, and in dug-out canoes – anything that would float – all the time with support from their aircraft, while our own planes had already disappeared from the skies. As the landing grounds on the island had been destroyed by Japanese bombing, their own aircraft were unable to land there, but on 13 February a British plane had landed on the main Kallang Airport road. Word went around that this had come to evacuate some of the General Staff to Java. The plane managed to take off after a very short run and that was the last any of us saw of British or Allied aircraft until 1944. The few remaining planes that had been left had been withdrawn, leaving the Japanese free to drop their bombs wherever they liked. This they did, day after day, soldiers and civilians suffering alike. As well as bombing the airfields, they bombed the island's naval base but, not content with that, they also targeted the centre of the town, where most of the population were Chinese. Day after day, down from the sky would come thousands of pounds of death and destruction. Backed up by heavy artillery, the Japanese pushed further into the island, seemingly intent on destroying everything and everyone in their path. They gained control of the Allied fuel and ammunition supplies and, crucially, the island's water supply.

Our situation was deteriorating rapidly. The numbers of our sick and wounded were increasing every day, and the chances of getting them away were nil. All the hospitals were full, and our injured filled other buildings, too, such as the churches, the post office and government buildings; everywhere lay wounded people – in corridors, basements and verandas, in fact, in every available space. More and more Japanese were working their way down the island. Streams of mud-covered men moved along the roads and through the parks, which had become battlefields. We moved up to a higher position to make another stand, this time with bayonet and knife. For a while we were able to hold them off, but they came again. Everyone needs to sleep at some time, and our chaps were no exception, but the only ones who slept were those who died: the sleep from which there is no awakening. More and more men were failing to come back from the patrols. The chap who had been at the side of me earlier hadn't made it back; now there was just an empty space.

We were then given news which, for a while at least, lifted our spirits. An order was received from the new General Headquarters in Java to the effect that we were to hang on, that reinforcements and supplies were on their way and that, at all costs, Singapore must not fall. The news was passed around all of us and we sent up a huge cheer, believing that at last our appeals for help had been heard, and answered. The Japanese must have thought us mad; there we were – no water, little food, and sleep out of the question, and yet all of us cheering in the middle of the night. By this time, of course, we had very little to hang on with but, encouraged by the belief that help was on the way, hang on we did. When morning came, each of us eyed the clouds, waiting for the sight of Allied aircraft, hoping we wouldn't have too long a wait. Nothing. The only aircraft we saw were Jap spotter planes with the by now familiar insignia of the Rising Sun on their wings. We scanned the horizon out to sea. Nothing. As the hours passed and daylight faded, so did our hopes.

As the morning of 15 February dawned, we felt even more desperate for the much needed reinforcements to appear, but they didn't. Above the town, thick black smoke filled the sky, the smell of burning in the air. The heavily populated parts of the Chinese quarters had taken a pounding. Still we searched the sky for our planes. Still nothing. Maybe we needed to cling onto that hope simply to keep ourselves going. We knew our position was poor, but who amongst us could have guessed that these were to be our last hours of freedom for three and a half years?

That evening, my pal Jim and I had just taken a couple of the chaps to one of the buildings being used as a casualty station for the wounded when word came to us that a 'cease fire' had been heard in parts of the town. We dismissed this as rumour, but later in the evening it was officially confirmed. Just hours earlier our thoughts had been on reinforcements but now, here we were, being told that it was all over. As hopeless as our situation had begun to seem, I couldn't take in this news at first. It just didn't seem real. Everything seemed to take on a hazy quality as my mind struggled with what was happening. I felt that my whole world had been torn apart and that nothing would ever be quite the same again. The expressions on the faces of the other chaps around me were enough to let me know that I wasn't the only one who was feeling this way. All I could think was, 'what now?'

We were given instructions that all personnel were to hand in their arms to the Military Police, which served to underline the fact that what was happening was real enough. But still the idea of becoming prisoners was hard to accept. After a word with our Commanding Officer, Jim and I decided to see what the chances were of escaping. We filled our packs with a few tins of sausages, sardines and fruit and made our way to the dock area, hoping that we might be able to get a raft, a boat – anything that would take us away from the island. It wasn't long before we realised this was impossible. The only thing afloat was a small steamer which was trying to evacuate some badly wounded and a crowd of women and children. There was nothing else and our hopes of escape were quickly dashed. We were going nowhere. Overwhelmed by tiredness, and having had very little to eat for days, we decided to make the best of a bad situation and found shelter for the night in Fort Canning. Months later, Jim and I would look back on that night and agree that back then we hadn't really known what hunger was. We ate some of the food we had brought with us, and drank juice from one of the tins of fruit to try to quench our thirst. We had taken tins of pineapple from one of the bomb-damaged warehouses a few days earlier and had been using these to try to combat the lack of drinking water. We soon discovered there were side effects to drinking too much pineapple juice, but there was nothing else – an early lesson in doing whatever we had to in order to survive. There seemed no point in staying awake when we at last had the chance to rest, so we settled down for the night and slept on a pile of groundsheets in the back of a truck. Waking up the following morning we wanted to believe that what had happened the night before had simply been a bad dream. Instead we forced ourselves to once more face the awful truth. We gazed around us, horrified by what we saw as daylight broke. Black smoke hung in the air above battle-scarred buildings and bomb-damaged roads. And something else seemed to hang in the air too – silence. All the noise of the last week or so – of bombing and mortar fire, and of the shouts and screams amid the battle that had been going on – had been replaced by an almost eerie silence. In the last week the island had changed almost beyond recognition. Everywhere we wandered there seemed to be chaos; rubble and dead bodies in the streets, shops boarded up, others being looted, confusion and fear on the faces of many people, especially the Chinese, whom the Japanese were known to hate.

Later that day we were told that the following morning, 17 February, we were all to make our way to Changi Garrison, to the north-east of the island, which is where most of the Allied forces on Singapore were sent upon becoming prisoners of war. We were told to take as much with us as we could carry, and that we would be allowed a few vehicles to carry the larger stuff. Morning came and we set off towards Changi, about fourteen miles away, joining a steady stream of hundreds of men walking ahead of us, and followed by hundreds, and then thousands, more behind. It wasn't long before we saw something that told us much about the sort of people who were now our captors. In order to reach Changi we had first to go through the centre of the town, where there had been a large contingent of Chinese. It was clear that the Japanese had repeated the treatment they had earlier meted out in Nanking, Shanghai, Hong Kong and other Chinese cities, where rape and murder had been widespread. We soon discovered that their brutality wasn't confined to the Chinese. One particular image that remains burned on my mind is that of the statue of Raffles, the man who made Singapore the place it had been before the Japanese had caused it such devastation. Surrounding the statue were some railings, about five feet high, with a spike on top of each. As we passed the statue that morning, we saw that on top of each spike had been placed the head of a Sikh soldier. These chaps had put the greatest fear in the Japs, letting out blood-curdling screams as they supported us in the street-fighting. Another statue stood nearby, also surrounded by spiked railings, and each of these now held the head of a Gurkha. I felt sheer revulsion for those who could do this. We walked on, sickened by what we had seen. A march of fourteen miles is nothing at all for a proud army. We were feeling anything but proud as we trudged along with heavy hearts towards who-knew-what, watched over as we were by Japanese soldiers who had an air about them which seemed to say, 'come and bow down before us, your conquerors'. Jim and I had marched about nine or ten miles when, like some of the other chaps before us, we managed to get a lift in a car for the rest of the journey. As we entered Changi, we gazed around at the sea of bewildered faces belonging to the men who had already arrived. Now we truly felt like prisoners.

Chapter Two

Rice and more Rice

Changi was the first of many prisoner of war camps which were to be our home for the next three and a half years. Several thousand British and Australian troops had already converged on the Changi area by the time we got there; a mass of men and their gear, to say nothing of the lorries and other vehicles loaded with food, medical supplies, cooking utensils, bedding and other articles which it had been thought might prove useful in the days ahead. Men continued to arrive throughout the day, steadily shrinking the available space. The barracks complex was large by normal standards and had housed between three and four thousand men before the war. Now, into that same complex were sent around fifty thousand prisoners. The problems associated with concentrating such a vast number of people at Changi were obvious from the start. The barracks blocks could house only relatively few men. The rest of us had to contend with more makeshift accommodation. Some of the chaps were in tents, whilst some found the means to make their own sheds. Jim and I found accommodation in an Indian hut. I wouldn't go so far as to say that this sort of thing would provide the answer to the present housing problem, but we welcomed it and its one piece of furniture, an Indian charpoy (an Indian word for a bed), which took the place of chairs, table and beds for the two of us. We hadn't been there long when we sat down to our first meal of corned beef, sardines and biscuits (these were not sweet biscuits but hard army bread which had been baked twice – or *bis cuit* in French). It didn't seem much at the time, and it may seem an odd sort of meal to many, but not many weeks later we looked back on it as a banquet.

Because of the sheer number of prisoners they suddenly had on their hands, the Japanese allowed our own officers to take charge of organising both us and the camp as a whole. Our being prisoners of war didn't alter the fact that we were still soldiers, and our officers still maintained discipline. In a situation where so much else had changed for us, and where our minds were filled with uncertainty, the fact that we had that discipline helped us to function. For the first few weeks we didn't really see much of the Japanese and, as long as we stayed within the perimeter fence, we were allowed to wander around the camp. They made it very clear to us from the start that anyone discovered outside the fence would be shot, as this would be seen as an attempt to escape. We didn't doubt that they meant what they said. Shortly after our arrival at Changi, word had spread through the camp that the day before the Allies had surrendered the Japanese had rampaged through the island's hospital, shooting and bayoneting patients and hospital staff, even killing a patient on the operating table. This sounded so horrific to us that at first we had wondered if it was true, or if the facts had become distorted. But no, it was true enough, there was no exaggeration. It had been nothing short of a massacre of innocent people. With that in mind, it seemed quite obvious to us that they wouldn't have needed much of an excuse to kill any of us.

I soon witnessed for myself just how ruthless the Japanese could be. Early one morning I was woken up by the sound of lots of shouting. As I went outside the hut, I saw two Japanese army lorries parked a short distance away with about fifty young Chinese men on board. As the guards ordered the men out of the lorries and onto the beach, I could see that each of the men's hands were bound behind their backs and that each of them was also attached to one long rope. As I stood there watching, a party of Japanese soldiers carrying three machine guns arrived on the scene. All this commotion had brought quite a few of the other chaps outside the huts to see what was going on, and it became obvious that we were about to witness a mass execution. Having caught sight of us, the Chinese greeted us with the familiar saying, 'Hello Johnny, Japanese no ******* good'. By my side was an ex-rubber planter who spoke fluent Chinese, and we gathered from him that these men were members of the gallant Dal Force, who had fought so hard for us and performed many acts of sabotage behind the Jap lines. However, because they weren't wearing uniforms and were not regular soldiers, the Japs thought fit to kill them. Although they were well aware of their impending fate, they knelt before their executioners, facing them with the sort of fatalistic smiles which seem to be a part of all Chinese. By this time, quite a crowd of our men had gathered. Forestalling any ideas we might have had of trying to intervene, the Japanese trained one of their machine guns on us and told us to go back to our huts, the nearest of which was about a hundred yards away. From there we watched as this wholesale murder took place. When it was over, another lorry of armed Japanese appeared to

11

escort the firing party back to town, leaving the bodies of the Chinese on the beach. As soon as the soldiers were out of sight, we ran across to see if there were any survivors. There was one boy. We carried him back to our hospital, where he was given the clothes and identity of a Eurasian soldier who had recently died. For the others, there was no escape.

The idea of escape did, of course, cross our minds, but in reality it carried very little chance of success. Any attempt, either by land or by sea, would have meant travelling thousands of miles before reaching anywhere not dominated by the Japanese. To most of us, the idea seemed suicidal. And so, rather than focus on how to get out of the camp, we got on with the business of working out how to live within it. Sorting out accommodation was just the start. It was then a case of getting used to coping without even the most basic facilities. Our lessons in survival had begun, and I doubt any of us would ever take anything for granted again.

The camp itself was a mess, badly scarred by the previous week's bombing. Some of the buildings had been badly hit, there were bomb craters in the roads and debris scattered all around. To add to this, because the water supply had been damaged, we were limited to what little water we could get from the few serviceable wells and there was no running water. In order to overcome this to some extent, the Japanese allowed us to go down to the beach to fetch salt water back to the camp to be boiled. This served the double purpose of providing us not just with water, but with salt too, which was also very scarce. However, most of the water was for the cook-houses and the remainder, like food, was rationed to us. The lack of running water still posed very real problems, not least because it meant there was no proper sanitation. Ditches had been dug as latrines but to have so many people living in such close proximity in tropical heat with only this primitive form of sanitation was a recipe for disease on a huge scale. We immediately began work on tidying up the camp, which enabled us to search around for things which we could use to make life more bearable, and this task became part of our daily lives. We became very resourceful, getting tips from some of the Australians who were with us, who had been prisoners in the last war. They warned us about some of the obstacles we were likely to meet in captivity and, thanks to them, we were able to equip ourselves accordingly. We began to view all sorts of items which we came across in a new light, asking ourselves if they couldn't somehow be put to good use. For instance, although we had brought food and some cooking utensils with us, we had no cooking facilities as such, there was no power, and there were a great many of us to feed. So we scouted around for things which could be used to cook food in, finding new uses for all sorts of things, from empty tins and barrels to new dustbins – ideal for cooking for such large numbers of people. As the camp had no power, the only way to cook or even boil water was to collect enough firewood, and this was a major task from the very beginning. The Changi area comprised several square miles, and once the sources of nearby firewood had been exhausted, parties of men went further afield within the camp to collect it, chopping down trees, and sawing them up to bring back to the cook-houses. This sort of heavy work saw the invention of what became known amongst us as the Changi Trailers. These were former army lorries from which the engines had been removed and the bodies replaced with wooden platforms. They had ropes on the front and had to be manhandled by teams of four or five men, which was very strenuous work as there were often hills to overcome. They became the sole form of transport used in Changi, whether for hauling firewood or stores of rice when rations were drawn.

From the moment we arrived at Changi it had been decided that the food we had brought with us needed to be strictly rationed, since we had no way of knowing what the future held and how long it would be before we were given any more. Consequently, our meals were very meagre affairs, often consisting of no more than a couple of mouthfuls – maybe a biscuit or two, or perhaps a small slice of meat – and we were constantly hungry. After we had been at Changi for a week or so, with our own food stocks beginning to run low, we received our first rations from the Japanese. These consisted of rice, more rice, and very little else other than small quantities of tea, sugar, salt, oil and a few vegetables. For the rest of our time in captivity, rice was to become our main diet. To the British, the word 'rice' conjures up a vision of a home-cooked rice pudding baked to a nice brown on top, with nutmeg and sugar added. Our issue had no such pleasant connotations. Our rice diet did not come in dishes, but by the hundredweight (112lbs or 51 kilos) in sacks and, even in its uncooked state, was unlike anything any of us had experienced before and always contained more than a few maggots. I doubt that even a highly-trained chef could have concocted anything tasty from it, and we were rank amateurs in that respect. For the first few weeks, all efforts to make the rice palatable were unsuccessful, mainly due to the lime preservative which produced an odour which was anything but appetising.

Neither did it look very appealing – grey, glutinous and really quite revolting. The addition of salt helped, making it just about edible. In normal circumstances, I doubt any of us would have eaten it, but our circumstances were anything but normal and we were extremely hungry. And, of course, there was very little else, so choosiness was a luxury we simply couldn't afford. After many trials, we discovered that soaking the rice for a couple of hours eliminated much of the preservative but, of course, we were hampered by lack of water. As time went on, the cooks experimented with other ways of cooking the rice which did lead to some improvement, and were able to acquire things such as dried fish to add to it and thereby give it some flavour, but in those early days at Changi our meals were depressingly unpalatable. There were also some unpleasant consequences to this diet of rice and very little else, with many men suffering from diarrhoea and just as many suffering from constipation.

By the time we had been at Changi for a couple of months, we were in no doubt that the Japanese cared little about our welfare. We had used all the rations we had brought with us and were living solely on the food they issued to us, namely rice and a few vegetables. Not only did those rations fall far short of being enough to eat, they were of very poor quality and so contained very little goodness. Dysentery had already got a grip on the camp, largely due to the poor sanitation and the difficulty of keeping the flies at bay, and it was only a matter of time before vitamin deficiency began to seriously take its toll on us. This was only the start of the assault wrought on our bodies by malnutrition. Little did we know then that things were to become a whole lot worse.

The fact that we were always so very hungry meant that food and how to acquire more of it became something of an obsession. Sometimes this involved doing things we wouldn't ordinarily have done had we not been desperate. Therefore, if an opportunity arose to have a rare treat of meat, our need for food helped us to set aside any qualms we had about what this entailed, as Jim and I discovered after we'd been at Changi for about six weeks. We were sitting outside our hut one evening with a couple of other chaps talking about food, as we often were, when a huge ginger cat strolled past. All talking suddenly stopped and all eyes turned towards the cat, which looked a lot better fed than us. Jim said he reckoned that a cooked cat shouldn't taste too different to a cooked rabbit, that food was food and wasn't it worth finding out? In fact, he'd said what all of us had been thinking – food was indeed food – and the fact that this wasn't the sort of animal we would normally have eaten didn't alter that. In no time at all we had agreed this was an idea worth pursuing, and had worked out how we could provide ourselves with a hearty meal. I was elected to build an oven and cook the treasure once it had been caught, so I searched around for some old bricks and a few pieces of tin so that I could make an Aldershot oven, which was rather like a miniature Nissen hut to look at, with a detachable door at one end. The principle on which it worked was very simple: first of all, the materials for the fire would be placed inside the oven and lit; then, when the oven reached a high enough temperature, the fire would be withdrawn, the food put in its place, and the door would then be fixed in position, so that the food would be cooked by the heat retained in the sealed oven. It was important to give the food plenty of time to cook without opening the door to check, as this would allow the heat to escape and result in a half-cooked meal and the prospect of having to start the firing process again.

Two of the chaps began hunting for the cat that night, but in the event it was two days before they managed to catch it and prepare it for cooking. The oven was heated and in went the cat, along with a few handfuls of sweet potatoes, ginger root and a wild form of turnip, together with some coconut oil to cook it with, which we acquired from a lamp. As we waited for it to cook, there was an almost childlike excitement amongst us at the prospect of what we hoped would be a wonderful meal. It wasn't long before a very appetising smell began to draw attention. Friends appeared from nowhere, and a couple of chaps came over with a bottle of sauce which they said they were willing to swap for a tit-bit of whatever it was that smelled so good. After the cat had been in the oven for an hour or so, with great anticipation the door was removed and the dish taken out. There before us was the nearest resemblance to a roast and two veg that we were likely to see. Any misgivings we may have had about tackling this meal were soon proved groundless by our empty mess tins and satisfied sighs. We hoped that the cat was one of a large family with relatives living in the nearby vicinity but, in fact, this was merely the start of our experimenting with somewhat unconventional dishes. Whenever an opportunity presented itself, snake, iguana, hedgehog and lizard all helped to stave off hunger. The longer our captivity went on, the more apparent it became that, where food was concerned, you needed to be prepared to try anything, however much you might have instinctively recoiled from the thought of eating some particular animal or other. This was survival, pure and simple.

By this time, although there was still a great deal of uncertainty about whatever lay ahead, at least some order had been established out of the initial chaos and our days had some sort of structure to them. We were kept relatively busy during the day with camp duties, but during the evenings we would pass the time talking amongst ourselves and, invariably, the talk would be about how much longer the war would go on. Many of us had great faith in the Allies to bring an end to our captivity soon, and in those early days at Changi some had the end of the year earmarked for when this was likely to happen, which would see us home for Christmas. We had no idea at the time how wide of the mark this was, but even those who did not share this sort of optimism could appreciate the need to try to keep up morale. Of course, this wasn't always possible. Cut off from the rest of the world as we were, it was all too easy at times to imagine that we had been forgotten. Home seemed so very far away and, like everyone else, I sometimes wondered if I would ever see any of my family again. There was no way of knowing what they were going through and what the war was doing to them. And even if we had known, there was nothing we could have done about anything. We were powerless. There were several radios hidden in the camp and now and then bits of news would filter back to us to lift our spirits. Their location was known only to very few people because of the huge risks involved, the Japanese having made it known that anyone found in possession of a radio would be killed. Most of the time we felt very isolated, as though the world beyond Changi no longer existed.

What made our sense of isolation worse was the fact that we felt so completely helpless to do anything about our situation. There was a dangerous lack of medical supplies with which to treat the increasing numbers of men filling the camp hospital. Thanks to the thousands of flies which constantly buzzed around the latrines and the cooking areas and their efficiency at spreading disease, more and more of us were going down with dysentery, and as there were also considerable numbers of mosquitoes, the hospital was having to deal with several cases of malaria. We could feel ourselves going downhill physically. I think we all had bad days when a wave of despair would sweep over one or another of us, and this is where friendship played such a huge part in helping to get through another day, and then another week, another month and so on. Many of us had served together for some time before coming to Changi without having become firm friends, but sharing the hardships of captivity led to the forging of friendships which were invaluable, both in terms of the struggle to keep up morale and the struggle to survive, as the effects of malnutrition and disease began to take their toll. Jim and I had known each other since we joined the Army back in 1934 and had rarely been apart since. Now that we were PoWs, whatever hardships we faced, we faced together. If one of us managed to acquire some extra food, we shared it between us. If one of us had a particular problem, we shared that too, as far as possible. But we had also become quite good pals with some of the other chaps too in a way that perhaps wouldn't have happened had we not been taken prisoner. Thrown together in these primitive conditions (though they were to become a lot more primitive before long) and having to live on our wits, there was an overall sense of us all being in the same boat; every one of us was hungry, every one of us was vulnerable to illness, and every one of us was anxious about what the future held. We were helpless to do very much at all about any of those things, but one thing we could do was help each other.

Chapter Three

Working for the Japanese

A few weeks after we arrived at Changi, the Japanese began to put some of us to work outside the confines of the camp in working parties, engaged in clearing up the island. Parties from twenty to fifty strong left the camp, some going to the docks, others to the airfields, and the largest party of all – known as the 'Shrine Party' – made their way to Bukit Timah, where they were put to work building an enormous shrine in honour of the Japanese dead. Often the working parties were used to move supplies of food from warehouses which had been damaged during the bombing, or loading ships at the dockside, and these were looked upon as golden opportunities for getting hold of extra food.

My turn came on 1 April 1942, when Jim and I were detailed to a working party going to MacArthur Camp, which had previously been used by an ambulance unit. When the Japanese had worked their way through the island a couple of months earlier, this place had been the scene of bitter fighting, the evidence of which was still all around. When we arrived at the camp, we were met by the sight of dozens of badly decomposed bodies lying on the ground. Our first task was to bury these poor souls with as much ceremony as we were allowed to muster. These had once been people, with families, loved ones. In our eyes, common decency surely demanded that their remains be treated with some dignity. However, it soon became apparent that this was not a sentiment shared by the Japanese. We hadn't seen that much of them in the time we had been at Changi, as our own officers had responsibility for the running of the camp, but now that we were working elsewhere on the island, the Japanese were more of a presence, and we were learning quickly that they were not to be underestimated in their capacity for brutality, their total disregard for the welfare of their prisoners, and their lack of respect for human life in general.

The daily routine in this camp was quite a departure from what we had become accustomed to at Changi. Each day we were taken by lorry to work at various different locations, the first of which was a bomb-damaged pineapple factory, where some of us spent several days moving thousands of tins of pineapples. A few tins managed to find their way back to the camp, where they were shared out between us. As wonderful as this treat was, one of the chaps remarked that it would have been all the better for having some custard to go with it – a simple enough idea but, of course, beyond our means at that time. It seemed to sum up how far removed we were from the simple pleasures of life – things we had no doubt taken for granted before we had become prisoners of war – and it was a moment that stuck with Jim and I; now and again, when faced with far too little food, or food that was particularly unappetising, we would tell ourselves that one day we were going to eat our way through a wall of custard and no-one was going to stop us! Our work at the pineapple factory was followed by a couple of weeks working at brickyards and foundries collecting salvage for the Japanese, which was later shipped to Japan. After a month or so, some of us were sent to work at the Hume Pipe Company, where we dismantled all serviceable equipment and machines (sabotaging them whenever we were able to, of course), which were also destined for shipment. We were then sent to the former Ford works, where we did much the same thing, stripping cars of their parts so that these too could be shipped back to Japan. By the time this salvage work was completed, there was very little left in the coffers of Singapore.

At the end of our second month in this camp we were put on the payroll of the Japanese army at the lordly rate of ten cents per day. This was paid to us monthly and, for thirty days 'coolie' labour we each received the equivalent of one shilling and three pence. Back home, this paltry amount would have been something worth taking up with your trade union. Where we were, of course, trade unions would not have been much use, as the only 'strikes' the Japanese recognised were those performed with the butt of a rifle and were not to be encouraged too often if you were to survive. This small amount of pay was still enough to make a difference to us, however, as we were able to use it to supplement our rations by purchasing food from the Chinese and Malay hawkers. This undoubtedly allowed us to have a few more vitamins and, perhaps just as importantly, it helped lift our spirits a little.

We spent another couple of months at this camp engaged in much the same sort of salvage work for the Japanese and then, on 8 August, Jim was sent back to Changi as a casualty when an ulcer which he had had on his leg for some time became very troublesome owing to lack of attention and medical supplies. There were no facilities at this camp for treating anyone who was sick in any way, and no compassion for them from the Japanese, which meant no pay either if they weren't well enough to work. Jim was just one of several who were sent back. The Japanese viewed us solely as workers. If we were unable to work, we were of no value to them; to be of no value to them was to be very vulnerable – something which became all too clear as time went on. The hospital at Changi had already been very low on drugs and even the most basic medical supplies when we had left in April and the Japanese had refused to provide any, but at least Jim and the others who went back had a chance of recovering with the help of the doctors there, who worked so very hard for us. What neither of us knew when he left was that we wouldn't see each other again until February 1945.

Shortly afterwards, I was detailed to another working party of a hundred and sent to a camp at Pasir Panjang. Working with us at this camp were chaps from the Malayan Volunteer Units. These units were after the style of our own Territorials and were largely made up of British and European estate managers and businessmen from all over Malaya. The accommodation at this camp consisted of two rows of single-storey stone buildings which had previously been used as coolie lines, and one wooden hut, which was about sixty feet long by twenty-five feet wide. The Volunteers occupied the stone buildings, whilst the hundred of us moved into the hut, which is where we slept and had our meals. It seemed strange without Jim, but at least I had already got to know a couple of the chaps in this party from having worked with them previously. We had become quite good pals, helping each other out in one way and another, and this was the

24

case for most of us, wherever we were. Friendship was very important; it meant that you didn't feel you were going through all this alone. We were very much going through it together, propping each other up, sometimes literally. There were exceptions, of course – men who were driven by hunger to steal food from others, for instance – but, by and large, we looked after each other. However bad things were, I've no doubt they would have seemed worse without some good pals looking out for you.

At this camp, our main occupation still involved moving things from one place to another, for the benefit of the Japanese, obviously, but this time it was the loading and transportation of oil and petrol from the main tanks to the docks. Once again, this sort of work provided opportunities for getting the better of the Japs now and then, which always gave us a tremendous boost. It meant taking risks, and some of us did get into a spot of bother once or twice, but we always weighed up the risks beforehand and, generally, it was worth it to have a go because it helped to keep our spirits up, especially if it resulted in our acquiring some extra food. It helped a great deal that not only did the chaps in the Volunteers have lots of local knowledge which proved very useful to us, but they also helped us to overcome any language difficulties in our dealings with the local traders.

After we had been at this camp for a few weeks, the Japanese High Command issued some forms which they wanted us to sign, on which it was stated that we gave our honour not to attempt to escape. These forms were to be signed by the men back at Changi and elsewhere on the island as well, not just those of us at this camp. However, the British GOC protested strongly against this on the grounds that it was against international law, and refused to comply. There was a stand-off for a couple of days but the Japanese then presented an ultimatum to the effect that if the agreement was not signed by all concerned, our rations would be reduced to starvation level, beginning with those of the patients in hospital. In the face of this, the British administration in Changi gave instructions that the agreement was to be signed in order to prevent further hardship to all of us. After this was done, we were given to understand by our GOC that having given our word under pressure we were not bound to keep it in the event that an opportunity arose for us to escape.

As the end of 1942 approached any optimism we had felt in the early weeks of our captivity that our ordeal would be over by Christmas had long since faded. With Christmas just weeks away, there was no sign at all as far as we could see of there being any breakthrough on the horizon. The thought of Christmas inevitably made us think more of home, and we wondered if our families knew where we were, and even if we were alive. If we were thinking of them, they were bound to be thinking of us. Jim and I had spent several Christmases together and always managed to have a laugh but we hadn't been PoWs then and Christmas in captivity was bound to be somewhat different. As well as the Volunteers, there were eighty of us out of the original hundred left at the camp by this time, the others having returned to Changi due to sickness. There was general agreement amongst all of us that we should try our hardest to make the best of things. We knew the Japanese were unlikely to make any concessions to it being Christmas, and that in itself seemed reason enough to do what we could for ourselves to mark the occasion. It was always a boost to our morale whenever we managed to find a way to achieve what we thought of as minor victories, usually involving illicitly obtained goods. It helped to counteract the fact that the Japs tried so hard sometimes to grind us down, often seeming to delight in tormenting us about food. They knew, for instance, that due to the pitiful rations we received we were permanently hungry, and yet at meal times a popular pastime of some of the guards was to open a tin of corned beef (which had formerly been British rations), eat a mouthful, then place it on the ground in front of us just after we had finished our tiny ration of rice and tea. After a few minutes, the flies – huge bluebottles, far bigger than the average house fly – would settle on the meat and lay their eggs almost immediately. Once this had happened, the Japanese would tell us, usually with a smug look on their faces, that we could have the meat. To do this to men as hungry as we were was a deadly form of torture. No doubt it would have given the guards great pleasure had we taken the meat, as anyone who ate it would have been guaranteed to contract dysentery, but we had more sense than to give into temptation.

We realised that if we were to get any enjoyment at all out of Christmas as guests of the Japanese we would need to eat something other than rice, which still formed the major part of our diet. The challenge was in acquiring it but, all things considered, we did quite well. Between the hundred of us we managed to secure, in various quite devious ways, four chickens, one duck, five fish (species unknown, but similar to cod), about twenty pounds of whitebait, a hundredweight of mixed vegetables and some fruit. We even acquired some coffee, though only a very mild form of it. Those tasked with the preparation and cooking of this lot did us proud and, to us, it seemed a real feast. The day was to be remarkable in another respect because the Japanese not only gave us half a day off, they also gave us ten cigarettes and a felt hat each – riches indeed! However, we later discovered that this wasn't generosity on the part of the Japs as these items had been sent by the South African Red Cross.

We rounded off our first Christmas Day in captivity by holding a boxing tournament that evening – Volunteers versus Regulars – the outcome of which was victory for the Volunteers. My personal gain amounted to two black eyes, which unfortunately became the cause of a misunderstanding the following day between a member of the Imperial Japanese Army and myself. When I woke up on the morning of Boxing Day, my eyes felt quite sore and I couldn't see properly, so I reported sick. The Japanese in charge of the company, who was in one of his nastier moods, ordered all sick personnel to parade before him. He then proceeded to investigate the causes of our sickness. When my turn came, he asked what my trouble was, although this was quite obvious, due to the bruising and swelling around my eyes. I replied that I could not see well enough to work. However, when he discovered that I was able to see his hand when he held it close to my eyes, he called me a liar in a choice selection of English and Japanese and then did his best to add a cauliflower ear and a broken nose, which qualified me for a day in bed and the loss of my ten cents for that day. So much for Christmas 1942.

On 27 December, our working party returned to Changi, to discover that during the nine months we had been away there had been many changes, and the whole Changi area had been reorganised. This had been carried out by our officers, who were still responsible to the Japanese for our behaviour and the manner in which we carried out our duties, and for the daily routine, but the Japanese grip seemed to be tightening. Changi had been divided into five camps – Australian, Dutch, Eurasian, combined British and American, and one for the hospital – each with their own perimeter fence; in effect, five camps within the overall area of Changi, which comprised several square miles. In order to travel from one camp to another, we had to pass through a barrier guarded by members of the Indian National Army, who were now with the Japs. These men were, for the most part, deserters from the Indian Army, but some had been forced to join. Each day, when working parties of men were detailed to go from one camp to another for various reasons, a British officer carrying a red flag would march at the head. Many of the Indian sentries stationed at the barriers took advantage of their position and at every opportunity humiliated both officers and other ranks by demanding a salute, often using the butt of their rifle to speed matters up. Not surprisingly, whenever such incidents were reported to the Japanese authorities, it was to no avail.

Now that we were back at Changi, there was a more settled routine to our days. A typical day started with reveille at 0600 hours, followed by a roll-call, or 'tenko' at 0615. This was carried out by the Japanese, who demanded an account of every man in the camp so, for instance, cooks who were preparing breakfast had to leave whatever they were doing and report and, in some cases, men who were sick had to be carried to the parade. Following this, at 0700 hours, we would have breakfast, which generally consisted of rice porridge flavoured with a teaspoon of locally produced sugar, a mug of unsweetened, milkless tea, and a salted fish resembling a kipper. (We had taken our tea without milk since the early days as milk was very scarce and what little there was went directly to the hospital.) After breakfast, the camp had to be cleaned. At 0800 hours, with the exception of those who were sick or who, for some reason or other, were excused working parties, the whole battalion were paraded by the WO or NCO on duty and detailed into parties for the day's work. Then, at 0815 hours, the working parties would be marched off to their respective locations, which included the wood yard, the rice stores, the battalion gardens, and the huts where the day's rice had to be ground. At 1030 hours there would be a tea break. The tea would be of the same colour and taste but there would only be half a mug this time. Then, at 1045 hours, work would resume until midday, when we would have our midday meal, usually consisting of a bowl of rice and fish soup, followed by a bogus roly-poly made from rice flour and peanuts, helped on its way with the usual neat tea. At 1400 hours there would be organised games and P.T. for all, apart from those who had not completed their work and then, at 1630 hours, we would have our tea, which seldom varied from one small slice of rice bread and a piece of fried pumpkin. By this time, the mug of tea would be rather anaemic, as the same tea leaves would have been used for each brew. The person who said that the first cup of the day is the best was surely right! At 1700 hours we would have to attend another roll-call so, once again, everyone had to parade. At 1800 hours we would have our supper, which was the high spot of the day. If the Messing Officer had been fortunate at the main canteen, there would possibly be vegetables and a larger piece of fish with the eternal rice. And, on a very lucky day, there would perhaps be a spot of jam to spread on the slice of bread. By this time the tea would be looking weak and tasting even weaker. Following our meal we would be allowed to make our own amusements providing they were not detrimental to the Imperial Japanese Army. Sometimes groups of us would gather for a smoke and a chat, often about whatever the current rumours were, or about the latest news from the two secret radios which were concealed in a trench, though few knew of their exact whereabouts and they were only in operation two nights a week, owing to the difficulty of recharging batteries. These gatherings also brought us news of the internees in Changi gaol, contributed by the tree-felling parties who worked in the woods opposite. By this time there had also been much effort put into devising ways to combat the inevitable monotony of life in a PoW camp, and at least once a week, entertainment was provided by a theatre and boxing ring which had been constructed in the centre of the camp, and there were also cinema shows of the silent 1920s era. They were all welcome distractions and then, at 2200 hours, it would be lights out on another day. One nearer to release, we hoped.

Although there was much about our existence at this time which was still very difficult to cope with, some of the changes which had taken place did bring about a degree of improvement to our lives. For one thing, the gardens which had been established were proving to be a rich source of food, producing such treats as sweet potatoes, spinach and pumpkins, and also tapioca root, which tasted similar to potato when cooked. These not only added some very welcome variety to the endless rice, but also some much needed nutrition to our vitamin-deficient diet. For another, we now had rice-grinding machines, which enabled us to make rice flour. This meant that it was now possible to bake small loaves of bread, to make puddings and also a kind of porridge. We had attempted to grind rice by hand in the early days at Changi, but it hadn't worked very well. These machines, however, did the trick. They resembled mangles, and worked in much the same way; the rice was put through the rollers until it was reduced to a fine enough powder to be used as a substitute flour. We also discovered that if we roasted this flour it gave off a smell similar to coffee, and we even managed to make a slightly coffee-tasting liquid from it; not a patch on the real thing, of course, but a change from very weak tea, or water. And at least we were now able to drink water more freely, since the water supply had been restored and we no longer had to resort to boiling seawater. Also, there was now a canteen, where we were able to spend our hard-earned pay. It was run by a camp welfare committee, who kept the prices of things within our means. We were able to buy peanuts, coconuts, dried fish, gula-melaka – which was rather like syrup and made from locally produced sugar – and, very occasionally, some toffee. This canteen committee was also responsible for the purchase of extra food in the town, the cost of which was borne by a subscription from each man working of one dollar a month. We were also able to buy food from a few Chinese hawkers who were allowed inside the camp.

All these things undoubtedly helped, but only so much. The fact that we were paid so little meant that we couldn't afford to buy very much and this led us to devise all sorts of other ways in which to make money. This was certainly the case with a scheme dreamt up by one of the Australians, who was put in charge of a steamroller. Although this machine was run on wood and coal, he managed to draw petrol and oil for it, which he then sold to the Chinese, purchasing food for his section from them with the proceeds. He was able to get away with this for about six months, until the Japanese finally discovered his profitable sideline. They beat him up rather badly but he maintained it had been well worth it. By this time, black marketeering had become rife, thanks to the opportunities which came our way whilst on working parties. One of the chaps had quite a lot of money and bought a substantial amount of tobacco on the black market. He then enlisted the help of a few friends and together they spent the evenings making cigarettes. These they put into packets made from scrap paper, on which they even drew their own brand design. When a few hundred packets had been prepared they set out to sell them in the camp at twenty cents for a packet of ten, and the whole lot sold in a very short time. For the second batch, two extra men were employed to assist in rolling the 'smokes' and, again, the stock went very quickly. Thus, the originator of the scheme made what was, to us, an enormous sum. The last I heard, he was employing fifteen men to do the work whilst he sat back and received the money.

Even though we had discovered various ways of adding to the meagre rations given to us by the Japanese, malnutrition was still very much a problem, and many of the chaps were suffering from deficiency related diseases. Various forms of dermatitis were becoming common, causing the sufferers great discomfort and, in some cases, agonising swelling to various parts of the body. Also, increasing numbers of men were going down with beriberi, largely as a result of the lack of vitamin B in the diet. This disease took various forms, some of them very serious, but those suffering from it often had grossly swollen feet and lower legs, as I was to discover for myself some time later. Those of the chaps who had, like me, spent several months on working parties at various places on the island had been able to take advantage of the opportunities this work presented for acquiring extra food and this undoubtedly made a difference to our health because we had been able to get more vitamins than we would otherwise have done. The men who remained at Changi for the whole time hadn't been so lucky in this respect. And, of course, the men who were unable to work due to sickness didn't receive any pay, so didn't have the means to buy food and get some extra vitamins, although many of us were happy to share what we had with them whenever we could. After all, none of us knew when it would be our turn for the hospital. The fact was, in the eyes of the Japanese, if men didn't work, it wasn't worth wasting food on them, even if they died as a result. The numbers of men being admitted to the hospital had risen steadily over the months and there had been several deaths which, under different circumstances, would have been avoidable. As it was, there was often little that the doctors could do as they had so little to work with. Sometimes we were able to buy some medical supplies from the local traders but it was never enough. Men were dying and the Japanese cared not at all. In the months I had been away from Changi, an English and Australian cemetery had been laid out. When I had my first sight of it I was struck by how much at odds it seemed with its surroundings. It seemed such a quiet and peaceful place, with wild flowers growing over the whole area – an oasis of calm amid the commotion of camp life. Each grave was marked with a wooden cross which bore details of name, rank, number and regiment, and a Roman Catholic chapel had been built nearby with materials salvaged from

34

various damaged buildings. Even at that point, some nine months after we had become PoWs, there had been many absolutely needless deaths, and yet things were to get so much worse.

Chapter Four

A Journey into the Unknown

A couple of months after I had left Changi in April 1942, the Japanese had sent an order to the British headquarters to the effect that several thousand prisoners were to be moved north to Thailand in order to simplify the problem of food distribution. It was understood that the camps these men were going to would be of the convalescent type. To substantiate this, permission was given for the men to take with them their recreational gear and whatever musical instruments they had. The first party of around three thousand men left Singapore in June, followed by another group of between two and three thousand in October, and several thousand more in November. After a while, news filtered back to Changi that these men had not gone to convalescent camps at all, but instead had been put to work by the Japanese on the construction of a railway which, when finished, would run between Thailand and Burma. The fact that much of the land in the railway's path was dense jungle and, therefore, very difficult terrain to have to work in, had deterred others from attempting to do this some years beforehand, but it didn't put off the Japanese. They considered this railway line to be essential to their plans as they needed an efficient way of supplying their forces in Burma and, with so many prisoners at their disposal, they saw us as the ideal labour force. Consequently, whilst thousands of men were sent to Thailand to work on the southern end of the railway, thousands more were sent to Burma to work on its northern end.

When I had returned to Changi in December 1942 I had hoped to see Jim again, but I discovered that he had already been sent to work on the railway, having left with the second group the previous October. From time to time bits of news got back to us about the conditions the men were having to deal with there and we began to realise that although there was much about life at Changi that was bad, by all accounts things were much worse for those who had left for Burma and Thailand. I spoke to a couple of chaps who had been sent back to Changi having tried to escape from one of the camps on the railway. They were in the hospital recovering from the combined effects of malnutrition, exposure and ill-treatment upon being recaptured. What they told me about the kind of work they had been doing left me under no illusion as to the so-called convalescent camps. They were fortunate in that they survived to tell the tale, as many others who attempted escape in the months and years which followed did not.

In March 1943, I left for Thailand as part of what was referred to as 'D' Force, which was comprised of thousands of British and Australians. On 23 March we were taken to Singapore railway station and saw that we were to travel in metal goods trucks. The journey itself was a nightmare. Thirty of us were piled into each of these trucks, which measured approximately 18 feet long by 7 feet wide by about 7 feet high: thirty men, plus our kit, bedding, stores and cooking utensils, plus one of the Japanese guards and two bundles of their kit. We were packed in so tightly that it was obvious from the outset that things were going to become very uncomfortable. Sitting down was possible only if we sat on our kit. Lying down was out of the question, and so was sleep. The trucks had a central door on each side which we were only allowed to have open about 12 inches, and all the necessary functions of nature had to be performed via these doors. Hour after hour, the journey went on, and the further we travelled, the less bearable it became. Thirty men crammed together in a small space in a hot climate for a long time, with nothing to eat, nothing to drink and no toilet facilities. Day turned into night and before long this metal box in which we were trapped, which had felt unbearably hot just hours earlier, began to feel very cold. On we went, mile after mile, into another day and in the heat of the sun the truck once more felt like an oven. It wasn't until the afternoon of the following day that the train made a brief stop and we were given something to eat, which was rice (of course) together with some sort of stew, and a small amount of water. Everyone was desperate to get out and walk around but no-one was allowed to leave the truck except for two men who acted in the capacity of mess orderlies.

Within an hour, we were on our way again. The air inside the truck was foul: all of us badly needed a wash and some of the chaps were suffering from dysentery. Those who managed to fight their way to the doors in time had to do their best to aim outside while a couple of us kept hold of them to stop them falling out as the train rattled along. Not everyone managed to make it to the doors in time. Another day and another night passed, with just the one stop for food and too little water. This time we were allowed out for a short time to relieve ourselves. After this brief chance to stretch our legs, it was back into the truck, the inside of which became more and more unpleasant as the journey wore on. We had no way of observing any kind of hygiene, no way of keeping clean. Since the beginning of our captivity a little over a year beforehand, for all that our pride had taken a hell of a knock and we had had to put up with all kinds of deprivation, we had managed to hold on to our dignity. The train journey to Thailand finally took a large chunk of it.

After we had been on the train for three days we pulled into Alor Star, where I had been stationed for a year prior to the fall of Singapore. From the door of my truck I saw the same old Sikh stationmaster. He recognised me and gave me a guarded smile, but I didn't speak to him as I knew that, if I had done, there would have been reprisals for him from the Japanese. However, he did manage to send a coolie over with a boiled egg for me. Such a small thing, but it was good to know a simple act of kindness amidst the horror of everything that was happening. The moment was soon broken by the jolting of the train and the noise of the Japanese guards and, once more, the journey was resumed. Before long we were in Perlis, the last Malayan state before reaching Thailand. We had travelled several miles into Thailand before realising that the border had been crossed, as we hadn't seen any frontier signs. Our first intimation of this was the presence of Thai soldiers and police who thronged the first Thai station at which we stopped. This was Ban Pong, the junction for Bangkok. We knew that for some of the men who had been sent to Thailand before us, this was where their train journey ended, and that a camp had been built nearby, where they had spent a short while before going further north to work on the railway. However, the Japanese had other plans for us. The Malay engines were replaced by Japanese ones, which I was to become well-acquainted with later, and within a short while the train began to move again.

The stretch of railway we were now travelling on had been built by the chaps who had got here before us. From Ban Pong to Kanburi, which was our destination, was a distance of about forty miles, but it took us another day and a half to cover it. This was because the embankment had not had time to settle and in many places the line had dropped by as much as two feet. In total we had to make nine halts, but at least this meant that we got to smell fresh air and stretch our legs, as during three of these halts the trucks had to be manhandled over the bad patches of line whilst the engine went on ahead. Finally, five and a half days after leaving Singapore, and having covered well over a thousand miles, we drew into Kanburi, which was the end of the line as far as our journey was concerned.

Exhausted after the heat and filth of the journey, and having had virtually no sleep since we left Singapore, we emptied out of the train and began to make our way to the camp, about half a mile away. What a sorry sight we must have looked as we trudged along through the thick mud. We had been prisoners for just over a year and during that time we had all lost a lot of weight; each of us probably weighed at least two stones lighter than when we had first arrived at Changi. Our filthy clothes, or what was left of them, were hanging off us, and we had nothing to replace them with. Lack of energy, and the intense heat – it must have been well over 100 degrees – made that half mile to the camp seem much further, not that any of us were keen to get there. After the hell of the journey, no-one was banking on whatever awaited us at the camp necessarily being any better. That element of uncertainty – of never really knowing what lay in store at any stage – was one of the hardest things to deal with, because we simply had no control over anything that happened to us.

The camp was situated on the edge of what had previously been a landing field for aircraft. There were eight long huts, each constructed of bamboo with a thatched roof of dried palm leaves, or attap. Each of the huts held roughly two hundred men but even with a few more squeezed in, the majority of our party were still left without accommodation and had to use groundsheets to improvise some sort of shelter for themselves on the few patches of dry ground available. We soon discovered that camp conditions were very basic, but by this time we had learned to expect nothing else from the Japanese. It quickly became obvious that there were not enough latrine trenches to cope with such a large influx of men and that more would have to be dug. However, just as there were not enough huts for everyone to sleep in, such matters were not considered a priority by our captors.

We were told to make our way to the cook-house, where a meal had been prepared for us, and we were each given a rice and meat rissole and a mug of hot tea, minus milk, as usual. Like everyone else, I was so hungry by then that I would probably have eaten whatever was on offer, recognizable or not, but what all of us really wanted more than anything else right then was to sleep; to give our bodies a rest from the crippling tiredness that made every step such an effort, and our minds a rest from the sheer awfulness of the previous few days. However, sleep was to prove difficult. In place of beds, our sleeping quarters in the huts were two long platforms raised about two feet off the ground, which ran the length of the hut, one at either side. These platforms were made from split bamboo which had been hammered flat and clearly hadn't been built for comfort. With so many of us crammed into a hut, each of us had no more than perhaps 21 or 22 inches as our bed space, giving us very little room to move as we lay side by side. We were at least able to stretch our legs out, something which had been quite impossible whilst on the train, so, as soon as we were able to, we settled down to what we hoped would be a much needed sleep. However, our hopes of a restful night were soon dashed by the arrival of swarms of mosquitoes and night flies, both of which made sleep impossible unless you were completely covered, and that would have been unbearable on account of the heat. To add to this discomfort, the bamboo platforms were home to more than a few bedbugs, which made their presence felt throughout the night. One way and another, we were more than glad to see the dawn, as the insects then abated, but before the day was very old we discovered that, whatever else Kanburi might be, it was certainly no rest camp.

After our restless night we were more than ready to answer the call to breakfast when it came, and made our way to the cookhouse. We were given a meal of boiled rice and peanuts, a piece of rice bread and a mug of tea. Having had so little to eat since leaving Singapore, we were famished and all of us kept a watchful eye on the NCO in charge of rations in case there were any second helpings, or what became known to all of us as *leggis*, the Malay for 'more'. Few of us would have considered ourselves language scholars but I doubt there would have been a man at any camp on the railway who wasn't aware of the meaning of this word,

43

such was its importance to us. As time went on, we often wouldn't bother to sit down to eat our tiny portion of food but, instead, would squat or stand in the vicinity of the cookhouse so that if '*leggis* up' was shouted, we were close enough to get some. There were always plenty of takers, and there would be a rush from all sides to queue up for whatever was going, however small the portion. When you're quite literally starving, every little helps.

At 0830 hours the whole camp had to parade before a Korean guard whom we later learned was commonly known as The Undertaker, having apparently been responsible for the deaths of at least three men, probably more, and the hospitalisation of numerous others. Once we had assembled before him, he told us in very broken English that we were here in Thailand to assist in the construction and completion of the Thai-Burma railway. He then said that any men who were either drivers, engineers, clerks or cooks should fall out to one side so, being a driver, I joined this group. Those men who did not fall into any of these categories were then marched away to where some trucks were standing on the line, about half a mile from the camp, and we later discovered that they spent the remainder of that day unloading digging implements from these trucks. Four Korean guards then approached from the office and took charge of the respective parties. The cooks were marched away out of the camp, the engineers were taken to the Japanese workshop, the clerks were taken to one of the huts which was used as sleeping quarters, and those in the driving party, including me, were taken to a tool shed. I had foolishly imagined that, being as I had previously worked as a driver and was well acquainted with vehicle maintenance, these skills were to be put to good use in some way or another or that, at the very least, whatever work I was given would in some respect be related to vehicles. How wrong I was. The driving party were instead introduced to the *empie*, which is the Japanese word for 'spade'. Each man was given one of these and we were then escorted across the aerodrome, through the town and down to the banks of a fast running river. This was the Kwai Noi, and the railway we were charged with building ran parallel to it. The river banks were formed of heavy ballast and for a moment, as I stood looking down at the stones under my feet, I was reminded of Brighton beach, but the resemblance to it stopped there. Running along the bank were three sets of lines, each holding approximately twenty trucks. At the first set of trucks we were halted by the guard, who then explained to us that, as we were drivers, our job before returning to the camp for our next meal was to drive the *empies* into the ballast and load the trucks. I resolved at that time never to volunteer my services as a driver again unless I had seen the vehicle which was to be driven! However, on our return to the camp we discovered that the men in the other three parties hadn't fared any better than we had; the cooks had been put to work cleaning out the Japanese cookhouse, peeling vegetables and carrying water, the clerks had been on hut-building duties, and the engineers had been kept busy unloading wagons of engine oil. The whole business of segregating those of us with particular skills from the main body of men seemed to us to have been quite pointless.

The following day, a small group of men were detailed to stay at the camp to dig trenches for latrines and to begin building huts for the many who had had to camp out on the ground, but the Japanese said that in future this work would have to be done after we had completed the day's work on the railway. Camps were built along the line like this as the work on the track progressed, but work on the railway always came before hut building, and even then the first huts which were built were those which were for the use of the Japanese, once again leaving us in no doubt as to how low down our welfare was in the overall scheme of things. With the exception of the hut-builders and a few others who were allocated to cooking, the rest of us were detailed to various work parties on the line, and so began the daily routine that was to become so horribly familiar to thousands of us over the following months, at this and countless other camps. Each day after a meagre rice breakfast (hardly the sort of stuff to set us up for a hard day's physical work) we would have to parade before the Japs and wait while they counted us and detailed the work parties. We would then make our way to the tool sheds where we would collect whatever tools there were for the job in hand, such as picks, shovels and axes. Considering that we were there to construct a railway track some 250 miles long, the tools provided for this task were somewhat primitive and mostly of very poor quality, which didn't make things any easier. However, we knew that things were even worse for some of the chaps working further up the line because the track was to go through some very difficult terrain where they were and like us, they only had the most basic tools to work with. Whichever work party we were on, we were constantly under pressure from the guards to keep working. Despite the difficulty of working in the heat and the fact that we were already weakened as a result of our poor diet, there was no let-up; there was always a Jap ready to shove us in the back with a rifle or a bamboo pole if we showed signs of slacking. We were allowed a break for a meal – usually a portion of rice and a drink of tea – at lunchtime and, depending on the work we were doing, this would either be brought out to us, or sometimes we would return to the camp for it. The only other breaks allowed were when the engineer called for a *yasmee* or 'rest', when we would get a ten-minute break and another drink of tea. We would then work until 1730 or 1800 hours when, after parading for roll-call once more, we would make our way back to camp, tired, dirty and hungry, to another meal consisting mainly of rice, with perhaps a small portion of very watery stew with a few pieces of vegetable floating in it. However unpalatable the meals were, it was vital that we ate whatever food there was if we were to survive, because the weaker we became, the less chance our bodies had of fighting the various diseases which were already claiming lives. After we had eaten, we had a few hours to ourselves before settling down for the night, and as we had managed to rig up some coconut oil lamps, at least we didn't have to sit in pitch dark. Often there was very little to do in the evenings so it was down to us to find ways to combat boredom. Sometimes there would be a quiz, other times we would take it in turns to talk about some place or other we had been to, and sometimes we would even find ourselves laughing about something or other, which at least proved to us that we still had a sense of humour, as awful as our situation was.

Now that we were actually part of this huge workforce, the true scale of what the Japanese were trying to achieve had become very real, as had their determination to achieve it. The railway was to be a supply route for Japanese troops in the north and they were totally focused on it, whatever the cost in human lives. Our first few days at Kanburi were enough to teach us that building the railway, and building

47

it quickly, took absolute priority over everything else. Quite simply, it was the only thing that mattered. It mattered more than any other kind of work, and certainly more than the welfare of those being used to build it. Those first few days also showed how very different life for us was going to be at this camp compared to Changi. Not only were the conditions back there not nearly as harsh as those we now faced, but, having seen comparatively little of the Japanese at Changi unless we were on a working party, we were now constantly under the watchful eyes of the guards. We had already seen how easily they could be provoked to extreme anger when one of the chaps had been bashed with a rifle butt for failing to stand completely still on parade at roll-call. We had also seen how the guards sometimes needed no provocation whatsoever to lash out at someone. Not all of those guarding us were Japanese; some of them were Korean, but they had no official rank in the Japanese army and clearly resented this fact, so appeared to try to compensate for it by making a show of wielding their obvious power over us. Working on the railway also brought us into contact with the Japanese engineers who, although they were in uniform, were not actually soldiers, but it was they who were in charge of line construction.

For the first few weeks I was mostly detailed to the party doing line packing, which involved packing ballast around the sleepers to hold them in place. It was monotonous work, occasionally made more interesting by the fact that we would sometimes be sent as far as seven miles from the camp, riding on the line in small petrol-driven trolley-cars. Korean guards oversaw our work on this party, and we learned very quickly to be wary of them because of their brutality. I was then taken off this job and detailed to a tree-felling party at a site some four miles north of the camp, quite close to the line. This job also entailed clearing undergrowth, including thick bamboo and, like everything else, was all done by hand. Japanese guards accompanied us on this party but it was the Japanese engineers who were in charge of us here, and we found them to be a little more human than the Koreans, not least because sometimes they allowed us an extra *yasmee* in the afternoon if work had progressed well. At times like this, when we worked several miles from the camp, our meals – the usual rice and tea – would be brought to us. Each working party which left the camp for the day was accompanied by one or two men whose job it was to provide tea for the *yasmees*. This job wasn't always the easy number that some thought it to be. It entailed having to carry a couple of four-gallon cans and the rations of tea from the camp to the work site, making a fire and seeing that the tea was ready for whenever the Engineer called for a *yasmee*, which doesn't sound too bad. However, it was sometimes necessary to make numerous journeys to the river to get water for the tea and sometimes this was quite some distance from where we were working. There was also the problem of collecting wood which was dry enough to keep the fire going – no easy task in the monsoon season – and then, at the end of the day, carrying the heavy tea cans all the way back to camp. And with this job, just as much as any other, if a guard thought you weren't doing it fast enough, or well enough, he'd let you know in no uncertain terms. The fact is, because our health was deteriorating so rapidly and we had so little stamina as a result of our poor diet, there were no 'easy' jobs on the railway; they all felt hard work. Without doubt, some jobs were worse than others, and I think we all felt for those who were having to do them, whilst also

49

being well aware that it could be our turn next. Wherever we were on the railway, we were treated as no more than slave labour.

Whichever working party we were on, we were constantly goaded by the guards. Often they would bark out orders to us in their own language, which we stood little chance of understanding and then, if we didn't immediately comply with whatever they had said, they would lash out with whichever weapon was nearest, often a bamboo pole. Trying to reason with them simply made matters worse; there simply *was* no reasoning with these people. If one of us was getting a beating, it was a case of just letting him take it. If anyone tried to step in to help one of their pals, they would get a beating too and things could, and sometimes did, quickly escalate to the point where the punishment meted out became one that was out of all proportion to the original so-called crime.

One of the incidents I witnessed at Kanburi showed this only too clearly. During roll-call one morning, the British orderly sergeant informed the Japanese NCO that there would be ten men less that day for the ballast working party because these men had badly blistered feet and were unable to walk. He asked if they could instead be given some work of a light nature in the camp, whereupon the Japanese NCO ordered them to appear for inspection by The Undertaker immediately. Four of the men had no boots and the others were unable to wear theirs because of the condition of their feet. For some reason this enraged The Undertaker, who seized the first thing which came to hand – a broom handle – and proceeded to beat the men about the head and body. Two of the men ran into the nearest hut, closely followed by Korean guards, who brought them back.

Another, an Australian, landed a very nice right-hander on The Undertaker's chin and floored him. Our first thought upon seeing this was that it was a good show on the part of the Australian, but the price he was made to pay for retaliating like this was a lesson to us all. We watched as he was tied to a tree near the Japanese guardroom, where he was left in the blazing hot sun without food or water for forty-eight hours. As much as we hated not helping him in some way, we knew without doubt that if any of us did so we too would be given this punishment. After this time, he was taken by truck to the rear of the camp, where he was made to dig a hole big enough to lie in. Having done so, he was shot by one of the guards and buried in the hole. A couple of days later an English padre was taken to his grave for the purpose of seeing that he had been decently buried. The excuse the Japanese gave for shooting the Australian was that he had attempted to escape which, of course, was completely untrue. His 'crime' had been to cause The Undertaker to lose face by hitting him and that, in the eyes of the Japanese, was unforgiveable.

A few chaps did try to escape, and invariably paid with their lives. A drummer from my own regiment had attempted to escape through the jungle but was captured after four days and brought back to Kanburi. He was tied to a pole outside a Japanese hut and left there for over twenty-four hours, with no food or water, and we were powerless to help him in any way. Then he was made to dig a hole in the ground measuring about 6 feet long, 2 feet wide and 2 feet deep. Once he had finished, he was made to kneel by the hole and was beheaded by a Japanese officer. All we could do for him was fill in his grave and erect a bamboo cross, with his name, rank and number. Another needless death.

Now that we saw so much more of the guards, we did our best to weigh them up, to try to detect any individual traits which marked any of them out as being better or worse than others. If we had to live among these people – and, clearly, we had no choice – we reckoned that, in the interests of self-preservation, we needed to try to understand what made them tick so that, hopefully, we could use this to our advantage. From what we had seen in these first few weeks at Kanburi, the general consensus among us was that the Korean guards were the worst for callousness and downright cruelty. As for the Japanese, it was generally agreed that the best of them were the uneducated ones, who would sometimes ask us questions about England and about our families, even asking to be shown any photos we had. By conversing with them in this way we were able to gradually pick up a little of their language, which was to prove useful as time went on as it enabled us to understand conversations which were not intended for our ears. By contrast, the educated Japanese considered themselves to be far superior to us and, as a result, were by far the worst of the Japs to deal with. They seemed to feel the need to prove their superiority by imposing punishments for the slightest reason, or even for no reason at all, simply because they could. For all their supposed superiority, there were times when we were able to show them just how ignorant they were, and their resulting anger proved to be anything but civilised.

Living as we were, at the mercy of people who cared not one iota about us, it was quite uplifting on the rare occasion that a little kindness came our way. One day as we began to make our way back to the camp after work had finished, I was taken quite ill with what I later discovered was an intestinal type of colic, very much like sprue. I collapsed in pain, my stomach extremely bloated, and just lay on the ground, unable to continue the journey back to camp. After a couple of kicks had failed to get me to my feet, the guards accompanying us must have decided I wasn't going anywhere and the rest of the party carried on without me. After a while, I became aware of a shadow over me. I opened my eyes to see a Buddhist monk and a young novice of about ten years of age. The monk bent down, felt my swollen stomach and then spoke to the boy, who then ran off somewhere. Shortly afterwards the boy returned carrying two things – a copper bowl containing some sweet-tasting liquid, and a parang, which is a knife with a large, curved blade. After giving me the liquid to drink, the monk raised the parang and, to my horror, brought it down on my distended stomach. What I hadn't realised as I saw the parang come down was that he had reversed the blade so that the wide back of the cold piece of steel was the part that touched me. Immediately, the pain lessened, as a combination of shock and the touch of cold steel caused my system to release the trapped wind, and an hour later I was able to walk again. When I looked around, both the monk and the young boy had disappeared, so I was unable to thank them, but experiencing that sort of kindness when there was so much indifference to our welfare and so much about our existence that was awful did much to help me retain some faith in human nature.

Chapter Five

No More than Slaves

Towards the end of May 1943, when we had been at Kanburi for about six weeks, our lives were made all the more difficult by the arrival of the monsoon season. No doubt as a result of being so exhausted at the end of each day's work, we had adjusted to sleeping on hard bamboo to the extent that we did at least get a few hours' sleep despite the best efforts of the bed bugs and mosquitoes. However, torrential rain meant that we now had to contend with water leaking through the roof of the hut as we tried to sleep. Had the Japanese allowed the hut-builders to use enough attap for the thatch, it would have been waterproof, but they always stinted on supplying enough materials to do a job properly. As it was, every hut had the same problem, resulting in the floor space inside becoming very muddy. Moving about the camp meant squelching our way along slippery paths, and the rain just kept coming. We would lie there at night listening to the rain splashing into puddles in the mud just below us. Some of us were able to keep relatively dry unless we happened to be directly underneath one of the leaky parts of the roof, but often the force of the rain would create a new leak in the thatch and begin splashing on our face or our feet and we would be awake in an instant. Some of the chaps had blankets to keep off the night chill but many of us had sold them in exchange for food. In place of these we had an assortment of sacks which we had obtained from various sources, some legitimate, some not. We opened the sacks at the seams and joined them together in order to get quite a large covering. For the most part, pillows consisted of pieces of wood and these had to be changed quite often on account of the bugs, which were impossible to get rid of and left their marks on us regularly.

Not everyone had the option of avoiding the rain and the mud for the entire night anyway; dysentery was rife, and there were always a number of chaps who had gone down with it at any one time. The awful thing about dysentery is that you can need the toilet dozens of times each day, and it doesn't confine itself to daylight hours. Those struck down with it who needed to rush out to the latrines during the night faced a slippery journey in bare feet through the mud, often in pitch darkness, and often more than once. To make things even worse, when the rain was at its heaviest, the latrines would overflow. Like many of the other chaps, before leaving Singapore I'd contracted dysentery a number of times. However much we had tried to be hygienic, taking care to wash our cutlery and mess tins and to shield the cooking areas from the ever present flies, this disease still somehow found a way to strike us far too often. Many of us had also had malaria at least once and, until medical supplies ran out, had been given quinine to help combat it. At the camp we were at now – and it was by no means among the worst of those on the railway – our living conditions were much poorer. There were easily as many flies and mosquitoes buzzing around us and as time went on, the ongoing lack of vitamins meant that we had very little resistance to infection and disease, but the medical officers could do little as they had virtually nothing left with which to treat anyone. Quite a few of the chaps had got terrible leg ulcers, with great, gaping holes in their lower legs. These had usually started off as just a tiny scratch, but as the infection took hold they got bigger and bigger and were often so deep that they went right down to the bone. Men were in agony with these ulcers which, in many cases, refused to heal because they were in such poor shape physically. Because of a lack of medical supplies, whereas the correct treatment for ulcers would have been sulphonamide, in most camps the most effective treatment was to place maggots from blowflies onto the wound so that they could eat away the dead flesh. Like lots of other chaps, I went down with beriberi whilst at this camp, and many of us also acquired skin diseases of one sort or another, and again, this was down to our hopelessly inadequate diet. Had the Japanese fed us better, then some of these diseases would have been avoided but, as it was, the rice they provided for us was of very poor quality, with no vitamin B content. This obviously affected our ability to function as a workforce, but rather than trying to restore our health so that we could work more efficiently for them, it became clear that they saw us as expendable; there were plenty more prisoners to take our place.

Shortly after the start of the monsoon rains, after yet another bout of dysentery had played havoc with my insides, I again fell ill with colic, and was in so much pain I couldn't stand, let alone work. The Japanese never showed any concern for anyone who was sick, and would usually hurl accusations of laziness and deliver a few hefty kicks if the chap was on the ground. After various attempts by the guards to get me to my feet failed, it was agreed that I could go to the hospital. This was actually quite a large hospital camp, situated about half a mile from the main camp at Kanburi, and consisted of long bamboo and attap huts, similar in construction to those we lived in, with bamboo platforms down either side for the patients to lay on. These huts housed not only those from the main camp who had contracted various diseases locally, but also hundreds from the working parties further up country. As far as possible, separate huts were allotted to those suffering from, for instance, malaria or those who had leg ulcers. There was also a small hut set aside for use as an operating theatre, where a mosquito net surrounded a makeshift operating table in order to keep insects off the patients' open wounds. This hut was the scene of many amputations and other operations, generally performed without the aid of anaesthetic. There were very few medical supplies left and the doctors had only the most primitive form of surgical instruments, but nevertheless managed to work wonders with items as basic as an ordinary butcher's saw, a dessert spoon and a razor. From the very beginning of our captivity there had been a need to improvise what we didn't have, simply in order to survive, and it became a way of life for all of us. As time went on, some of the chaps showed quite amazing ingenuity in the way that they managed to produce all kinds of things, including make-do surgical instruments, from metal containers, but even then there was always a great risk of infection, not least because the lack of dressings made it difficult to keep wounds clean and protected from the ever-present flies.

The treatment for my colic consisted of a pint of salt water four times a day and my normal ration of rice boiled to a sort of rice sauce, which we called 'pap'. After a week or so of this, I had recovered enough to walk about a little, so I was allowed to wander over to some of the other huts to look for old friends and acquaintances. I found a few, including a chap I had got to know quite well in the early days at Changi, who had been working at one of the camps further up country and was now recovering from a severe bout of dysentery and malaria. We swapped various bits of news and compared stories about our experiences of the camps and guards. From what he told me, it seemed Kanburi was no worse than any other camp, and the rumour was that conditions at the northernmost camps were much worse, with many deaths due to a combination of malnutrition and disease and, no doubt, ill-treatment because, by and large, the Japs didn't seem to know anything else. There was no getting away from the fact that they were, quite literally, working us to death. After another couple of days recuperating in hospital, I was well enough to return to the main camp and resume work. Shortly after this, the Japanese increased the pressure on us and I realised that I was lucky to have been allowed to stay in hospital until I recovered.

The beginning of the monsoon season had a huge impact on the progress of work on the railway. From our first days at Kanburi, we had been working for six to eight hours a day, often in intense heat and with most, if not all, of us suffering from malnutrition and a variety of deficiency diseases. Occasionally, if the Japanese considered us to have finished a particular task in good time, we would be given a day off, and those days were so welcome; a chance to rest our aching arms and legs and our sore feet. Then heavy rain began to hamper progress, embankments were washed away and had to be rebuilt, and as every surface became slippery underfoot – especially as many of us had nothing on our feet – it became much more difficult to move around. As a result, we were told that we had to work for longer each day and, against a great deal of opposition from our doctors, the Japanese began to demand that even those who were very sick should contribute to work on the railway.

From then on, our days began earlier. We had to have our breakfast and be on parade shortly after dawn broke. After we had been detailed to various working parties and drawn our tools from the tool shed, we would begin what was often a twelve-hour day's work and there were very few days off. We no longer went back to the camp for our meal at lunch time; rather, it would be brought out to us, so that we could resume work again as soon as our break was finished. Whichever kind of work we were doing, we were pushed to do it faster, and beaten if we were considered to be slacking. No allowances were made for those who were suffering with blistered hands or feet, or were weakened by repeated bouts of dysentery, or for those in pain from bad leg ulcers. Such things made no difference whatsoever to the guards, who delivered a whack with a bamboo pole to anyone they felt wasn't working hard enough. We were given to understand that Japanese powers on high had decreed that the railway had to be finished sooner than had initially been planned for. The guards were under pressure to see that this was achieved, and it was of no concern to them how many of us died in the process.

In order to boost their workforce, the Japanese had recruited thousands upon thousands of native labourers to work on the railway alongside us. Many of these were concentrated in the northernmost camps. These men had been promised good wages and conditions and plenty of food in return for working on the line, but were, in fact, treated even worse than we were. As a result of the appalling conditions generally in the camps, with so many men living in squalor with no proper sanitation, and with millions of flies buzzing around spreading germs, it was always only a matter of time before disease broke out on a large scale. This arrived in the form of a cholera epidemic. Word reached us that there had been a number of deaths among our men from this awful disease, but that very many more of the deaths had been among the native workers, who had little knowledge of hygiene or of how to protect themselves against this or any other disease. Of all the diseases we were susceptible to, cholera was the most feared and not just by us, but also by the Japanese. Cholera killed so quickly, and we knew that once you got it, there was no hope at all, and you would very soon be dead. So far we hadn't encountered it in our camp, but the fear was that as all the camps were located next to the river, the germs would travel downstream to us – something made all the more possible by the arrival of the monsoon season and the torrential rain which swept all manner of rubbish into the river. The Japanese cared about the welfare of the native workers even less than they cared about ours. Their attitude was that there were plenty more who could take the place of those who died. However, they were aware that cholera had the capacity to wipe out their entire workforce and so threaten the completion of the railway. As a result, they pushed us harder and harder to get the work done, seemingly oblivious to the fact that if they took better care of us by providing us with an adequate diet and with medical supplies, we would be in far better physical condition and therefore able to work all the harder. The increased workload meant that sickness claimed more and more of us. I doubt any of us would have been passed as fit for work under normal circumstances and most of us would have been hospitalised. As it was, the Japanese were reluctant to class anyone as unfit for work. As far as they were concerned, if you couldn't stand upright, then you could sit down and work, but you *would* work, and this sort of callousness had ceased to shock us.

We still sometimes found ourselves thinking about how we might escape from all this, but mostly we were realists, and we only had to look around us to be reminded of how unlikely it was that any attempt would be successful. Working in these unforgiving jungle conditions had shown us how hard it would be to survive for any length of time with only a few provisions, and that we would have to travel many hundreds of miles before reaching the sort of place where we would stand even a chance of blending in. What is more, although we would probably have been able to find some help among the Thai people, there would undoubtedly have been those in the native villages who would have been happy to turn us in. There was a price on the head of anyone who attempted to escape, and I don't use this term simply as a figure of speech; 150 dollars was on the head of every PoW who escaped and was brought in, dead or alive and, if this entailed a long journey, the natives had only to produce the head in a sack in order to collect their reward. Despite these risks, there were those among us who attempted to escape. One of them was a chap whom I'll call Joe, and though we admired his courage, his experience served to underline to the rest of us that any such attempt was little short of suicide.

For a month or so, Joe had been working down on the river bank, filling trucks with ballast, and during this time had become acquainted with an Indian whom he had previously known in Alor Star. Each day, during the *yasmees*, they had met secretly and planned their escape, gathering together what provisions they were able to. Several of us knew he was contemplating escape, but we had no idea when the attempt would be made. One evening as we paraded for roll-call before returning to camp, we were found to be one man short, but it was not until we returned to camp that we discovered it was Joe. For three weeks we heard nothing of him and wondered how he was faring, and only when he had been recaptured did we discover what had happened. On the day of the escape attempt, he had been working at the river bank as usual and during the lunch period had met his Indian friend, who was waiting with a boat, and together they had travelled up river for two days. Apparently, two Chinese guerrillas took over from the Indian, and the three of them then made their way on foot through the interior, heading for the Burma border. They then came across a Japanese convoy proceeding north along a jungle track, and managed to climb aboard the last truck unnoticed and hid under a tarpaulin, where they stayed until the truck stopped. Peering from underneath the tarpaulin, they found they were in the middle of a Japanese transport camp, but with very few Japanese in sight. They stayed hidden until nightfall but then, instead of continuing on their way as planned, the sight of so many unattended trucks proved too much for the patriotic Chinese, who were unable to resist the temptation to set fire to the camp. The guards were turned out and opened fire, wounding the Chinese, and leaving Joe to carry on alone. He was unarmed and without food or drink, as these had been carried by the Chinese. For the next two weeks he survived by living on fruit and what little he was given by friendly natives, but his escape attempt was brought to a swift end when he was suddenly confronted by a jungle patrol of Japanese.

Joe was taken to a Japanese military police camp and, having failed to give a satisfactory account of his presence in that district, was then taken before the *Kempetai* – the Japanese Gestapo, who were well known for being ruthless – and eventually returned to the camp. The first we knew of this was when a Japanese staff car drove into the camp one evening and a crumpled figure was pushed out and left sprawling in the dust – it was Joe. He was in a bad way and had obviously been given a good beating. For the next two days he was made to sit in the drain outside the Camp Commandant's office and none of us were allowed to go near him or to speak to him, and during this time he was given only two small bowls of rice. This punishment was punctuated by him being dragged inside the office and given the third degree by the Japanese in an attempt to discover the names and whereabouts of his accomplices, but Joe was too ill and exhausted by this time to even understand what was being asked of him. When the Japanese realised this, they went to the other extreme to try to ensure that he didn't die before they could extract this information from him. He was taken to the hospital and a British doctor was given responsibility for his wellbeing, which is how we learned of his story. On Japanese orders, Joe was given the best treatment and food available, even down to fresh liver, which the doctor said would accelerate his recovery. Once recovered, he was again subjected to questioning, but continued to refuse to divulge the names of those who had helped him and it wasn't long before, once more, he was in a bad state. He was due to be sent back to Singapore jail but his body could take no more, and he died and was laid to rest in Kanburi, safe at last from the Japanese.

Towards the end of June, new Japanese officers and guards arrived to replace those who had been overseeing us to date, whom we discovered were being sent to the Burma front. The new Camp Commander was Colonel Sijio Nakamura. Two days after taking over he inspected the camp and had a notice pinned up for us to read. The following is an exact copy of the original, worded in his unique form of English:

[A hand-written note of the following, dated 1946, was kept with the manuscript. Dad never mentioned it to me but I assume the note was a copy of an earlier copy of the original, made whilst at this camp.]

INSTRUCTION GIVEN TO POW ON MY ASSUMING COMMAND.

I have pleasure to lead you on the charge of last stretch of RAILWAY CONSTRUCTION WARDOM with the appointment of present post. In examination of various reports as well as to the result of my partial camp inspection of the present conditions, am pleased to find that you are, in general, keeping discipline and working diligently. At the same time, regret to find seriousness in health matter. It is evident that there are various causes inevitable for this end, but to my opinion, due mainly to the fact for absence of belief in Japanese 'health follows will' and 'ceases only when enemy is completely annihilated'. Those who fail to reach objective in charge, by lack of health or spirit, is considered in Japanese army as most shameful deed. 'Devotion till death' is good yet still we have the spirit 'Devotion to Imperial Cause even to the seventh turn of life in incarnation' the spirit which cannot become void by death. You are in act of charge in colleague with Imperial Japanese Army. You are expected to charge to the last stage of this work with good spirit by taking good care of your own health. Besides, you are to remember that your welfare is guaranteed only by obedience to the order of the Imperial Japanese Army. Imperial Japanese Army will not be unfair to those who are honest and obey them but protect such. You are to understand this fundamental Japanese spirit and carry out the task given to you with perfect ease of mind, under protection of Imperial Japanese Army.

Given to Kanchanaburi June 26 1943,
Colonel Sijio Nakamura.

Needless to say, this notice became the source of much discussion amongst us. The poor state of our health was, it seemed, our own fault; we should have to try harder, safe in the knowledge that the Imperial Japanese Army would protect us!

This new commander was, however, responsible for implementing changes which improved our lives to some extent, although some of his ideas did fall a little flat. For instance, he believed that prisoners benefited from indulging in recreation after work was finished for the day. This would have been a good idea were it not for the fact that everyone felt far too tired on their return to camp to participate in any sporting events. Often it was all we could do to drag ourselves back to the camp, wash away the day's dirt, and eat our portion of rice and watery stew before getting some rest. Few of us had the energy to do any more than spend a while talking amongst ourselves in the huts before settling down to sleep. By this time, fortunately, we all seemed to have acquired the ability to sleep through all manner of things which, in the earlier days, might have kept us awake – mosquitoes, bed bugs, the noise of the rain, not to mention aches and pains; exhaustion tended to overcome the lot most of the time, giving our bodies a chance to recover a little before they had to cope with another day.

Of much greater benefit to us was the canteen that this new camp commander was responsible for starting, as it meant that we were able to buy things like tobacco, fruit, oil and sugar at cheaper prices than those charged by the Thai hawkers who tended to line the camp boundaries every day. Since our arrival at Kanburi we had sometimes supplemented the poor rations given to us by the Japanese by catching lizards, snakes and monkeys to eat. We had so little meat otherwise that these tasted surprisingly good to us and, more importantly, gave us some much needed protein. At other times, we purchased food from the hawkers, though this often entailed selling something to them first. One or two of the more prosperous Thai and Chinese merchants were so confident of the outcome of the war that they changed an occasional cheque for those who had accounts in the two principal banking houses in the East, the Hong Kong and

Shanghai Bank and the Chartered Bank of India, China and Australia. Most of us, though, were dependent on the little pay the Japanese gave us and often the prices being asked were beyond our means. As a result, although we didn't have much in the way of possessions, there was little which was of more importance to us than food, and most of us had things we were willing to sell. The hawkers were always ready to buy personal items like watches, fountain pens or rings, as well as blankets, though many of us had already sold these by now. Although their offers were ridiculously low, with the money we made we were able to indulge in such luxuries as a few boiled eggs, *c'noms* – which were fried coconut biscuits – and Thai tobacco and cigarette papers. By this time, most of our clothes, including our footwear, had worn out due to continual wear, or was rotting as a result of seldom being dry since the monsoon season began, so few of us had items of clothing to sell. However, my boots, which I had been unable to wear for some time, still had a little life left in them. Sometimes now when I say that I would 'give my boots for a smoke', my mind goes back to the time when I actually did that.

Chapter Six

'Maintenance Specialists'

[Dad's next move was to a camp known to the PoWs as Wampo. The vast majority of the men sent here were housed in the main camp, but he was one of a comparatively small group who were based some distance away from this in a much smaller camp near the railway line at Wampo station.] He continues:

In August 1943 my time at Kanburi came to an end, when I was detailed to a party going further north. There were only a few of us in this party – two chaps from the Leicesters, one from the Gordons, one from the Norfolks, two from the RAOC, and me. The seven of us were taken to Wampo, at the 114-kilometre mark, a journey of about forty-five miles. We travelled there by way of a convertible army truck, one of several which had been adapted to enable them to run on the railway line; with their wheels removed, the hubs fitted the gauge of the line. Many small stations had been built along the line as work on the railway progressed. Each of them consisted of little more than a cluster of bamboo huts built alongside the line, equipped with a field telephone. Men were needed to keep these places clean, to chop and stack wood, draw water and clean the fires when an engine was taken off the run, and to do whatever else was deemed necessary. Every so often a party was detailed to move up country to do this work, and this time it seemed that it was our turn. We didn't know what to expect as a result of this latest move, although from the outset it had appeared to us to be a move for the better, but you just never knew. Our lives had become so unpredictable. We were, all of us, the property of the Japanese, to be moved around as their whim dictated.

Talking amongst ourselves, we soon discovered that each of us had a background in vehicle maintenance. The Japanese had taken note of any particular expertise men had a few months earlier at the last camp and, though it had subsequently seemed a waste of time when everyone was then detailed to the same sort of work, it now appeared things might be different. We soon found out this was indeed the case, when one of the guards informed us that we had been brought here to work as specialists in maintenance. Hearing this, we hoped that it meant we were considered to be useful and might be treated less harshly, although we were in no doubt as to our place in the whole scheme of things and weren't foolish enough to imagine that being useful made us indispensable; we knew there would be countless others who could take our places. For my part, although I'm not sure I would have described myself as a 'specialist', I felt very grateful that the Army made sure that, as a driver, you learned about the vehicles you drove. We all agreed that from what we could make of things so far, being sent here may well have increased our chances of survival. Deaths were occurring every day, with more men becoming seriously ill, and we all knew that any one of us could be next. We had been captive for about eighteen months by now and there wouldn't have been a man anywhere along the railway who was without some sort of disease or who didn't bear the effects of malnutrition. We had been among the thousands being worked to death either wielding picks and shovels, or moving earth, or clearing swathes of jungle, all by hand, whilst constantly being goaded by the guards. And then, quite suddenly, our little bunch had found ourselves removed from all that and sent to a much smaller camp. Perhaps it was luck. Or, as unlikely as it had seemed for all these months, maybe someone was watching over us after all.

Our living conditions here were similar to those at Kanburi in that although the huts were smaller, they were of the same bamboo and attap construction and we still slept on bamboo, complete with bed bugs and other insect life. Sanitation was still as primitive, with the same open trenches, often swarming with maggots. We were still fed the same small rations of low quality rice, and little else of any nutritional value and, as we sat down to eat it, were plagued by scores of the same fat bluebottles, ready to spread disease. We were still very much subject to the scrutiny of the guards, some of whom could be every bit as volatile as those we had encountered at Kanburi, and only too ready to hand out a beating if they thought someone had stepped out of line. (If someone did, literally, step out of line during roll-call, that in itself was sometimes deemed reason enough to warrant a whack.) There were, though, some crucial differences. For one thing, we were no longer living in overcrowded conditions; fewer people meant the potential for less disease being spread. For another, although we were still expected to work hard, we were no longer under the same sort of pressure, and nor did we have to endure the level of physical hardship that we had been subjected to for the previous few months. Added to this, although some of the Japanese guards seemed to delight in trying to make our lives difficult, there were no Korean guards at this station, and for much of the time we worked for the Japanese engineers, who were much more interested in getting the work done than giving us a difficult time. As a consequence, the discipline tended not to be as strict as it was at the larger camps.

Along with two of the other chaps, I began work in the engine repair shops, which were situated about a hundred yards to the rear of our huts. I soon discovered that this station was apparently quite an important place. It was here that the engines were refilled with water and where they were changed over, because from here onwards the gradient of the line became much steeper and two Japanese engines of the '56 Class' were needed to haul a load. I also learned more about the pressure the Japanese engineers were under to make sure they delivered a fully functioning railway. For instance, although the line was built as near as possible to the river, in some places the distance between the river and the line was two miles, something which the engineers were less than happy about. To overcome this problem, at stations every twelve or fifteen miles along the line, huge wooden tanks were built, which were kept full by way of two stage pumps down on the river bank. Not every day was spent in the repair shop as there was plenty of work elsewhere on the station, sometimes on line maintenance or repairing the embankments which the monsoon rains frequently did their best to wash away. Sometimes this entailed us travelling up and down the line on a breakdown wagon putting derailed engines and trucks back on the line. The Japanese still worked us hard here, but they didn't drive us as relentlessly. Even

Dad in 1935, aged 19, the year after he enlisted in the East Surrey Regiment.

Mum in 1941 during her training at the Royal Naval Hospital, Haslar in Hampshire.

Dad on guard duty in Shanghai, 1939, wearing service dress with webbing equipment. Note the puttees. He was serving with the 2nd Battalion of The East Surreys, who were moved to Malaya in 1940.

SIAM

Map showing the 250-mile long Death Railway from Ban Pong in Thailand (Siam) to Thanbyuzayat in Burma.

To Moulmein
Thanbyuzayat
Kendau
Wagale (8 K)
Thetkaw
Alepauk (18 K)
Kun Knit Kway
Retpu
Tanyin (35 K)
Beke Taung (40 K)
Anarkwan
Tanbaya
Kilo-55 Camp
BURMA - THAILAND
Mezali (70 K)
Meiloe
Kilo-80 Camp
Kilo-85 Camp
Kilo-100 Camp
Kilo-105 Camp
Kilo-108 Camp
Three Pagodas Pass
RAILWAY
Kilo-116 Camp
Kilo-131 Camp
Nieke
Taimonta
Upper Konkoita
Konkoita (274 K)
Krian Krai
Tamajao
Takanun (227 K)
Brancali
Kinsayok (188 K)
Hintok R. Camp
Hintok
Malayan Hamlet
Konyu R. Camp
Konyu
Tampie
Tonchan Spring Camp
Tonchan South (131 K)
Tarsau
Wun Yi
Wampo
Tamarkan (56 K)
RAILWAY
Kanburi (Kanchanaburi)
Chungkai
Tamuan
Wanlung
Bampong
Non Pla
Bar
Nakom Pa

Ye

BURMA

Menam

Kwa

Noi

THAILAND

River

Tavoy

100 KILOMETRES

PoWs at Changi, Singapore, where most of those taken prisoner at the fall of Singapore in February 1942 were initially held. It is believed that these PoWs were Australians.

Dad's Japanese PoW Index Card, which shows that he was transferred to the Thailand PoW Administration and became part of Work Group 2 on the Railway.

収 容 所 Camp	馬 來 昭和 17 年 8 月 15 日	番　號 No.	馬 奈 四　6974
姓　名 Name	O.X, Frederick	生 年 月 日 Date of Birth	6.7.16.
國　籍 Nationality	英	所 属 部 隊 Unit	No. 5110923 2nd East Surreys
階 級 身 分 Rank	Private 兵		
捕 獲 場 所 Place of Capture	SINGAPORE シンが 40.-ル	捕 獲 年 月 日 Date of Capture	昭和 17 年 7 月 15 日
父 ノ 名 Father's Name		母 ノ 名 Mother's Name	Ellen
本 籍 地 Place of Origin		職　業 Occupation	窓 装 飾 WINDOW DRESSER
通 報 先 Destination of Report	c/o 62 Squadron Royal Air Force, England	特 記 事 項 Remarks	

This photograph, taken just after the war, shows the track near Wang Pho (Wampo).
(By kind permission of the TBRC (Thai-Burma Railway Centre))

Another photo taken just after the war
showing the track and a train near Wang Pho.
(By kind permission of the TBRC)

The area around Wang Pho (Wampo) showing the dense terrain through which the railway was built. Photograph taken in 2003 by one of Dad's granddaughters.

Wang Pho station, photographed in 2003, close to the camp where Dad was held for over eighteen months.

The steel bridge at Kanchanaburi (Kanburi), on which Dad worked in 1945, photographed in 2003.

The Kanchanaburi bridge after Allied bombing in 1945.

The cemetery at Kanchanaburi where many of those who lost their lives on the Railway are buried, photographed in 2003.

St Peter's Royal Naval Auxiliary Hospital, Colombo, where Mum worked from 1942 to 1945. (By kind permission of Queen Alexandra's Royal Naval Nursing Service Archive)

The SS *Strathnaver*, on which Dad sailed home to Southampton in November 1945.

Mum and Dad's wedding day in January 1946.

Queen Mary's Hospital, Roehampton, where a special unit was established to treat those suffering from the long-term effects of captivity in the Far East.
(By kind permission of Queen Mary's Hospital Archive)

One of Dad's great-grandchildren placing poppies on a section of the original railway track at the National Memorial Arboretum, Alrewas, Staffordshire.

so, the work, combined with the intense heat and humidity of the day still left us very tired and drained of energy.

After our day's work was finished, a couple of the guards would accompany us to the river, so that we could have a much-needed wash. Then we would head back to the camp for our ration of rice and – on a good day – perhaps a rissole instead of stew (which was little more than water with two pieces of mushy vegetable in it if you were lucky). Because the railway embankment was repeatedly washed away in many places by heavy rain, we sometimes had to wait longer than usual for our supplies, which would be brought up the river by barge. This meant that by the time vegetables reached us they tended to be well past their best and beginning to rot. This was also often the case on those occasions when meat found its way to us, though we would still eat it if possible, as we were in no position to be choosy. After so many months of this totally inadequate diet, we had come to realise that the Japanese were unlikely to do anything to change this situation; they really seemed to believe that there was nothing wrong with providing working men with so little to eat and of such poor quality. As a result, we were still as obsessed with acquiring extra food here as we had been at the previous camp, as our bodies desperately needed more vitamins. Due to our poor diet, by now most of us had some sort of skin ailment and, like me, some of the other chaps had blurred eyesight from time to time, and this was down to vitamin deficiency. We were able to use our pay to buy some items of food from a native coffee hut which was located about fifty yards to the rear of the station and jointly owned by a Chinese and a Thai. Unfortunately, ten cents a day didn't go very far but we would buy what food we could, such as some fruit, brown sugar, perhaps some coffee, and also some native tobacco. Much as we needed extra food, we needed a smoke too! Fortunately, life at this camp offered us various opportunities – not all of them entirely honest – for adding to our diet. For instance, we become quite skilled at acquiring bananas from a nearby plantation. Choosing our moment carefully, we would enter the plantation as inconspicuously as possible, cut down a few stalks of bananas and then chop down the tree. This wasn't wilful damage on our part; we had discovered shortly after our arrival in Thailand that bananas do not grow on the same tree twice and that, to avoid detection, we needed to do as the natives did. Having collected his bananas, the native would immediately cut down the tree, and then plant a new shoot in its place as soon as the ground was fit, so if we had left the tree standing in its fruitless state, it was certain to have been noticed and we could well have found ourselves in serious trouble. We were also fortunate in that after we had been at this camp for a while the guards allowed us to make our own way down to the river to bathe. There was, after all, little chance of any of us attempting to escape, since there was simply nowhere to go that wasn't full of Japanese. This journey to the river, which was about half a mile away, entailed passing through a native village, the total population of which consisted of only two families. Much to our advantage, we became quite friendly with them, and they very generously quite often gave us food, such as fruit or dried fish. The kindness of these people meant a lot to us, and did as much for our morale as the extra food undoubtedly did for our health, and though our diet still had its shortcomings, we were no longer starving.

With the day's work over, in the evenings we would sit around having a smoke and discussing the day's events and sharing stories, often joined by Peggy, the bull-terrier mascot of the Gordons, who had travelled here with a chap known as Jock. He'd taken her under his wing from the early days of captivity and one of us would often take her ratting. She had to be closely watched when the Japanese were around, as she was none too fond of them and the feeling was mutual. She had a couple of run-ins with them but we became very protective of her. In fact, Peggy was treated as one of us, and however little food we had, we made sure she had a share of it. We found her being around us to be quite a comfort. The life we had been forced to live since we had been taken prisoner, and the things we had been forced to endure as a result had, to some extent, hardened us. There was so much death and disease, so much mindless cruelty and brutality. I suppose it was a case of having to mentally build a kind of wall around what you actually felt about these things just to carry on. But there was something about this dog being around us that let us know that we were still normal human beings, capable of normal feelings towards a helpless animal. I doubt the rats would have thought of her as being helpless, of course, as she was quite efficient at catching them!

Thanks to the monsoon, much of our recreation time was spent indoors, since the area outside was a quagmire. Had any of us still had any clothes or boots, we would have been hard pressed to keep them clean and dry. Some, like me, had sold their boots in exchange for something to eat or to smoke. Others had discarded them when the constant rain and mud had caused them to rot and fall apart, much like our shirts and shorts. Instead of proper clothes, each of us now wore what was known as a jap-happy – a piece of material about ten inches wide and about two feet long with a tape at each corner, which was worn between the legs and tied around the waist – and this presented no problem at all in drying. Walking and working barefoot in the jungle had left our feet sore and often bleeding so, like many of the other chaps on the line, we had resorted to making our own form of footwear, which were rather like clogs. They were made from two pieces of wood, which were roughly the shape of our feet, held in place by a thin strap over the toes. I wouldn't go so far as to say they were comfortable, and it was impossible to walk in the normal way in these, so we would shuffle along in them, but they were an improvement on bare feet. As a result, more than a few of us had fallen arches to go with the list of other ailments we continued to acquire as the months passed.

Our work at this station often enabled us to acquire news of what was happening elsewhere up and down the line, owing to the trains which regularly passed through. Day after day, trainloads of sick men were coming down from the north on their way to the hospital camps, and more loads of comparatively fit men (who, in normal circumstances, would themselves have been considered too ill to work) were travelling up to replace them. When the trains stopped at the station, some of us usually managed to get to them on some pretext or other, giving tea to as many of the men as we could, and replenishing their water bottles, trying to see if we knew any of those on board, and listening to the latest rumours from up and down country. We had already been aware of a cholera epidemic at one of the most northern camps, but just how bad the situation was up there was brought home to us when we heard that the victims were dying so rapidly that they were being buried twenty and thirty at a time, and that the epidemic had by now claimed thousands of lives, mostly Tamils, but some of our men too. As more trains passed through the station going south, we heard this same story again and again, except that the news got progressively worse. We heard that as cholera claimed more and more victims, the Japanese had resorted to burying some Tamil victims alive. We had no difficulty in believing that they would do this, having witnessed for ourselves the way they treated the native workers. The news was then of bodies being cremated rather than buried, in an effort to try to stem the spread of this dreadful disease.

One of the factors responsible for much of the disease was the total lack of hygiene in the native camps. The average native was simply not bothered if flies settled on his food and he would eat and drink from a rusty tin without giving a second thought to the fact that since he had last picked up that tin, which hadn't necessarily been washed, it would have been the playground of hundreds of flies. Those who had ulcers on their legs or arms didn't cover them, with the result that flies would settle on them and then carry the infection elsewhere. Nor did the natives take the precaution of boiling their drinking water and, when bathing in the river, would often take a drink at the same time. With all this in mind, it was little wonder that the cholera epidemic got out of hand. In our camps, we were scrupulous about hygiene. We took every possible precaution against disease and infection that our circumstances would allow. When our eating utensils were not in use they were placed upside down on a piece of wood and scalded with boiling water before they were used again. They were also periodically washed in a solution of permanganate of potash, which we also used to wash our fruit.

After we had been at this camp for about a month, we were told, much to our amazement, that as we were 'specialists in maintenance', from now on we were to receive thirty cents a day instead of the usual ten. To us, this sounded too good to be true, and we had long since learned not to believe a word the Japanese ever said. However, we did indeed receive this pay rise and very welcome it was too, as it allowed us to buy several little extras which we wouldn't otherwise have been able to afford, as well as a few more smokes. Shortly after this, at the beginning of November, we were detailed to build another hut, which was to provide accommodation for a party of men who were due to join us at the station. The fourteen of them arrived shortly afterwards, having travelled up the line from Ban Pong, where they had been working in a Japanese ration store. Ten of them were British, two were Australian, and two were Dutch and they were a welcome addition. It was good to see some new faces and hear the latest news from down the line. A few days later, another party of ten, all Dutch, arrived from Nong Pladuk and were also to be based here with us. In just a few days our little camp had become comparatively overcrowded. We wondered if more people had been brought here to work for a particular reason or if, perhaps, those of us who had been here for several months would be moving elsewhere. We knew we would be the last to know if that was the case, as there was rarely any warning of that sort of thing. As always, such things were beyond our control so all we could do was hope for the best. There had been another new arrival as well – a new Jap, who was now in charge of us and whom we nicknamed The Rat, and for good reason. He seemed determined to make his presence felt, and whereas life had fallen into some sort of routine in the previous couple of months and we had become used to those overseeing our work, he set about disrupting everything. Jobs that had been done once already had to be done again, this time to his liking. Roll-calls were conducted with a level of discipline we hadn't known before at this camp, because until the last couple of weeks, there had been few of us to count. Since we had come here, there had been fewer beatings, and those which we had received were usually the result of us having been caught in the act of doing something we shouldn't or being somewhere we shouldn't. More often than not this was to do with our quest for more food, and some of us did get roughed up rather badly once or twice, but there was less of the indiscriminate beating and less of the shoving in the back with a rifle or bamboo pole for no apparent reason up to now at this camp. With The Rat in charge, we realised things could change and became very wary of him.

It was hard to believe that another Christmas was drawing near. I think we all found it difficult to think about Christmas without also thinking about home. Some of the chaps had received letters from their families but many, like me, had none in all the time that we were PoWs. We reckoned that it was likely that the Japanese were stopping them from getting through to us, though there would surely have been no reason to do this. That was the thing though, with the Japanese – they just did things, and you could think and think about why and never come to an answer that made any real sense. We'd decided that it was often a case of them doing things simply because they could; they had all the power and we had none, and that was that. Being as we had no choice but to spend another Christmas as prisoners, we put our heads together to come up with the best way of getting through it in order to keep our spirits up. After much discussion, we decided that not only would we save our pay in order to have the best Christmas dinner possible, but that there were enough of us here now to have a concert party, as long as The Rat would give permission. Lots of the camps up and down the line had concert parties, and not just at Christmas, and they were a huge boost to morale. In the event, when The Rat was asked, he told us he would grant permission on two conditions: firstly, before it took place he was to be provided with details of what was on the programme in order that he could censor it if necessary; secondly – and much to our disgust – we were to use a Japanese tune for the Finale instead of our own National Anthem.

At the end of each day we worked on our plans for the concert party, which was to be held on Christmas Eve. Everyone was invited to take part or to get involved with it in some way or other, but most of the organising was done by those of us who had been there for some time, and I took the role of producer. It was good to have something to focus on, and I suppose as much as anything it was our way of showing the Japs – and maybe ourselves too – that despite our having been prisoners all these months, they hadn't broken us. As Christmas approached, the programme began to take shape, with nightly rehearsals held in the huts. We found that we actually had some quite decent musicians and singers among us. Music was to be provided by a couple of the Dutch chaps with their homemade guitars, as well as one of the British with his mouth organ. In addition, Bill, one of the Australians who became a good pal of mine, was going to sing Bush songs, two of the Scots were going to sing Scottish airs, and three of the Dutch were busy practising Javanese songs. Our star act was to be provided by one of the British, an English sergeant major, who was going to put on a puppet show featuring a boxing match. The puppets were to be attached to each of his arms whilst he crouched below the level of the stage, which was a crudely constructed bamboo platform surrounded by curtains made from sacks which had been dipped in red mud to dye them. After much coaxing, we managed to get the Japanese Quartermaster to agree to provide some lighting, in the form of two petrol lamps.

By the time Christmas Eve arrived, we were ready to put on a good show. Our nightly concert rehearsals had attracted the interest of the guards on several occasions and we had fully expected most of them to attend the performance itself. As it was, not only did all the fifteen Japanese who made up the station staff attend, but we were gate-crashed by about forty others – one and two-star soldiers who were spending the night in Wampo – plus about fifty natives, who spent the whole evening cheering everything. The puppet show proved to be an especially popular turn, and at the end of the performance the Japanese Commandant – much to my amazement – presented me, as the producer, with twenty cigarettes, which were shared amongst the cast. Such moments of good fortune were rare, so before anything happened to spoil it, we sat around to sample these. It was quite a change to taste a civilised cigarette, as these were Kooa brand, similar to our Woodbines and cost a dollar a packet. Our festivities weren't over yet, as on the evening of the following day we were able to have the Christmas dinner we'd saved for: a native dish called *samble*, which consisted of chillis, fat, onions, salt and sugar, fried and eaten with rice, together with some pigs' chittlings, followed by coffee and a cake made from rice flour, bananas, four fresh eggs (which had become a rare luxury at this time) and grated coconut. The sing-song we had afterwards was brought to an abrupt halt by The Rat shouting 'bugga, bugga, no goodo, all men sleepo', and 'ashita tuksun shigoto', which translated as 'all men sleep now, tomorrow plenty work'. Thus ended our second – and, we hoped, our last – Christmas as prisoners.

Chapter Seven

Stealing to Survive

With Christmas behind us, work was very much the order of the day and we began the new year of 1944 wondering what it held in store for us. Despite the efforts we made to keep our spirits up, we were all prone to having days when we felt quite overwhelmed by the bleakness of our situation, and fear and uncertainty about the future were never far away from our thoughts. For the last few weeks, although the Japanese still wore an air of authority that let us be in no doubt that they were the ones in charge, we had noticed that by and large they seemed less hostile towards us, less ready to lash out for no apparent reason. We wondered if this was something to do with the railway having been completed in October, months ahead of the original schedule but at the cost of a huge number of deaths among our men and the natives. Not that we thought for a moment that the Japanese would have been troubled by the thought of the vast numbers who had died so unnecessarily, as they had never shown any sign of caring one way or another who lived and who died. Rather, we thought that perhaps the guards were themselves being put under less pressure now and, as a result, were less inclined to put as much pressure on us. We had grown to be suspicious of every little change in their mood, and didn't trust them an inch.

Compared to the early days, there tended to be more Japanese at the camp now. It was not unusual for a Japanese troop train to wait at the station for several days before proceeding further north, and the troops would often nose around, ask questions and generally prove to be a nuisance, putting us on edge, especially if there were any Koreans among them. Since the completion of the railway, trains went up and down the line carrying not only rations, troops and ammunition, but also comforts for the troops, in the form of parcels and girls. The parcels generally consisted of a tube of toothpaste, a pencil, paper, postcards and – rather strangely, we thought – a doll. If I hadn't seen this for myself I would have found it hard to believe that a doll would be included in a parcel for a grown man, but seeing is believing, and what seemed even stranger to us was the fact that we had seen the Japs carrying these dolls around. We found it easier to understand their other form of comfort – Korean girls of questionable age who, having completed a tour of one camp, would pass onto the next, and so on up the line. On a couple of occasions we saw other females on the trains, but these were members of the Indian National Army. They were all young girls, dressed in brown shirts and skirts, each of them armed with a very old-fashioned bayonet, hanging from a belt at the waist, which we presumed was for self-protection. We learned that these girls belonged to a branch of the army the equivalent of our own ATS.

Before 1944 was very old I was detailed to work in the Jap cookhouse. I couldn't see how this fitted in with my being a 'maintenance specialist' but I was well aware of the obvious benefits to be had from such a job, due to the

84

potential for acquiring extra food. The combination of our being able to buy more food, thanks to our increase in pay, and to sometimes acquire it illicitly had certainly made a difference, but we still felt hungry most of the time. Each day's work left us feeling weak, no doubt because our bodies had been deprived of essential vitamins for such a long time, and so we continually craved extra food. Stealing from the Japanese was considered by them to be a serious crime, and was punished as such. We had all heard of chaps being given severe beatings for stealing mere scraps. I didn't see that as a reason not to do it but, rather, a reason not to get caught doing it. At first my work in the cookhouse consisted of peeling potatoes, washing out buckets and that sort of thing but after a while I was left to prepare some of the meals myself. This had great advantages as it gave me a chance to get some food over to our chaps in the evenings, enabling us to have regular nightly feasts of scraps of meat or fish, rice and, perhaps, some *samble*. Having been in this job for several weeks, I had learned which of our regular guards were the more vigilant and had a habit of nosing around the cookhouse and which ones tended to stay clear, and used this as the basis for deciding what I could get away with and when. Mostly it worked, but on one occasion I was caught on my way back to our hut carrying a bucket containing a few scraps. I proceeded to lie like a trooper in an attempt to get away with it, but it was clear from the expression on the face of the Jap who had caught me in the act that he wasn't totally convinced by the explanation I'd come up with. Apparently undecided as to whether I was telling the truth or not, he gave me a couple of very hefty clips around the ear and some very choice words, presumably in case I wasn't, but then let me go on my way. He wasn't one of our regular guards and was one of the largest Japanese I'd ever seen. When I finally reached our hut and explained what had happened, I told the other chaps I hoped that if I got caught again it would be by someone smaller! But we all knew that I'd been extremely lucky that things hadn't turned out far worse for me, as we'd seen men tied to a tree and left in the baking hot sun for an entire day for doing less.

A few weeks later one of the other English chaps called Ron joined me in the cookhouse. This made the process of stealing food somewhat easier as we were able to keep a lookout for each other when one of us was up to no good, at least in the eyes of the Japanese. Together the two of us plotted ways of smuggling food out of the cookhouse, but this was no easy matter. Had we worn clothes, we could possibly have got away with concealing things underneath them. As it was, all either of us wore was a jap-happy, which left nowhere to conceal anything. Instead, each of us would be ready with what we hoped was a good enough explanation if called upon to explain the other's absence for however long it took to do whatever was necessary. The thought of what we might be able to acquire in the course of our working day somehow gave us a sense of purpose and yet we sometimes remarked upon the fact that none of this should have been necessary, and indeed wouldn't have been necessary if the Japanese had seen fit to feed us properly. As it was, we had been reduced to the level of thieves and, what is more, thieves of often nothing more substantial than other people's leftovers. Mostly, however, we tended to think of what we were doing as simply helping ourselves and the other chaps to survive the ordeal of captivity, and we had discovered long ago that, whatever this entailed, it often left no room for pride; it was simply a case of doing whatever we had to.

As far as possible, any extra food we managed to get, we shared with the others in our hut. By now we had all become quite firm friends, sharing each other's ups and downs, and so there was no question of our not doing this. It would surely have been very selfish to have done otherwise, and I think we tried hard to stay the same sort of people we had always been, rather than let the Japanese and all their cruelty and neglect change us for the worse. There were times, however, when sharing things with the others wasn't possible. The ration trucks tended usually to arrive in the middle of the night, at which point Ron and I would be roused from sleep and made to unload them. Normally it was the case that once we had finished we would be accompanied back to the hut, so there was no opportunity to smuggle anything, but the job of unloading nevertheless had its compensations. The Japanese seemed to have an unlimited supply of eggs, but as it used to cost us thirty cents to buy one from the canteen, we weren't able to afford many, and they weren't the easiest sort of food to smuggle from the cookhouse. So, if ever we were presented with an opportunity to enjoy more, we took it. Taking care not to be seen, each of us would pierce an egg and suck out the contents, and then put the shell back in its place in the crate. The following day, if eggs were on the Jap menu, the eggs would be counted out into buckets and given to us to break and mix. We used to wait with bated breath for an empty shell to turn up and, when it did, the result was always the same. The Jap cook would shake the shell, realise it was empty and say, 'Thai chicken no good', whereupon he would throw the shell away and continue to count out the eggs, seriously under the impression that the chicken had laid an empty shell. Another minor victory to us!

Sometime around the end of May, our regular smuggling of scraps of food came to an end when Ron and I were replaced in the cookhouse by five Chinese – two women and three men. We had always felt that we should make the most of our time there while it lasted, and we had certainly done that, and I'm sure our health had benefited as a result. Ron was detailed to join the general labourers, whose work covered everything from hut building to digging bore-holes for latrines. Meanwhile, I was sent to the engine repair shops once more, where I worked alongside four of the other chaps from my hut. The workshop seemed busier this time around, and the engineers had plenty for us to do. As before, the guards were less in evidence here, which always felt like a good thing. We were given various jobs such as cleaning and packing the steam gauges, removing pistons, straightening buckled fire doors, washing out boilers and cleaning the fireboxes. The machinery in the workshop was all Japanese and consisted of a lathe, a drilling machine, a grinding wheel and a cutting tool machine, all of which were driven by power supplied by a Chevrolet engine mounted on a block. At one end of the shop a small but effective forge had been built and was in constant use. Just behind this was a space partitioned off where tools were kept under the very watchful eye of a Javanese, whose job it was to issue and collect the tools used during the day. Just outside the workshop and between the railway lines was a very antiquated inspection pit. Overhead was a bamboo and attap roof, underneath which were any engines which were being repaired or washed out. There were always a few cylinders of oxygen for welding jobs and, in the event that these ran out, a large carbon-burning apparatus was always at hand. There was less monotony to the days here compared with much of the work I had been detailed to do prior to coming to this camp and, having always been interested in machinery, I found the workshop quite interesting. Not for the first time, I considered that luck, or something or someone, must have been shining on me, as I could so easily have found myself among the countless other chaps who were suffering far worse conditions. Over the months, so many sick men had passed through the station as they travelled down from the north on their way to the hospital camps further down the line. Whenever we had been able to, we had tried to do what little we could for them by filling water bottles for as many as possible before the Japs could stop us, and in the process we had heard stories of such cruelty and callousness. Some of the men had looked as though they hadn't long left in this world. Some had legs missing, the result of ulcers not healing and leaving amputation as the only option. All of them looked as though they should have been in a hospital much earlier, rather than working on a railway line, but that wasn't the Japanese way of doing things.

All too soon the dry season, which had brought such a welcome relief from the seemingly endless rain, was at an end and once more we found ourselves slipping and sliding in our wooden clogs with mud squelching between our toes. Often a couple of us would be detailed to leave the workshop and go up the line to help repair an embankment that had washed away. We were doing this one day when it occurred to us that we had now seen the seasons go full circle at this camp. We had been here for over a year and were still no nearer to knowing when it would all end. Our main source of news here was that which we were able to pick up from chaps on the trains passing through. Mostly the news was of how things were further up the line, but occasionally we would hear something about the outside world, and, as time went on, we heard several rumours of there having been big advances in Europe. We were always rather sceptical when we heard something like this, something that sounded like good news. As much as we would want to think it was true, it was hard to know what to believe. However, we had heard these latest rumours from various sources so we began to think there might be actually be some truth in them. Each night we would sit on our beds, such as they were, and discuss the situation and what we would do when it was all over. The question many of us dwelt on was, 'when Europe is finished, will the Japs pack it in?' Opinion about this varied, but most of us were of the belief that the Japs would fight on, regardless of the numbers against them, as we had seen for ourselves how fanatical they were in their worship of the Emperor Hirohito who, it seemed to us, had the power of life and death over every being in Japan. On top of the rumours about Europe, we then heard that the Allies had begun bombing the line in Burma and that much damage had been done. This really was something to make our hearts beat faster. It seemed to us that what we were hearing was too specific to be mere rumour. Each day we would scan the skies, hoping to see a plane bearing the Allied insignia but, as had been the case when we had searched the skies above Singapore, the few planes we did see were Japanese.

Because of the state of the ground outside during the monsoon season, outdoor recreation was impossible, so instead we had to pass the evenings in our huts. At least here we were able to stay dry despite the heavy rain as we had managed to carry out repairs to the roof of our hut when we had been on hut-building duties to accommodate the new arrivals some months earlier. However bad things were, they were always made worse if water was dripping through the roof. We found various ways of trying to relieve the boredom and to generally keep up morale, and it was important to keep occupied because not doing so allowed too much time for thinking. Quite often a group of us would organise a spelling bee or a quiz. One night, we had just finished our evening's entertainment and were settling down to sleep when one of the chaps in the next hut came running in with the news that, as he was passing the station office a few minutes earlier, he heard one of the guards say the words 'hokoki Tampin'. Great excitement had then broken out among the Japanese, because these words meant 'aircraft at Tampin'. All thought of sleep was forgotten and we ran outside the hut to see if we could hear the sound of an approaching aircraft, because Tampin was a matter of only fifteen to twenty miles away. Our imaginations began to run riot, with each of us thinking we could hear planes, first from one direction, then from another. Eventually, a guard was sent over with instructions to see that we were all kept to our huts. Each minute seemed like an hour as we strained our ears for the only sound we wanted so much to hear – the sound of aircraft. Time passed. Nothing. We began to despair, and after half an hour or so a few of the chaps crawled onto their beds. The rest of us decided that sleep would have been impossible anyway after this excitement and sat listening for that sound to come, praying for it, almost willing it to happen. The strain we had been under for so many long months as prisoners suddenly felt as if it was more than we could take any longer; it felt as though we'd reached breaking point. The minutes ticked silently by. Still nothing. The guard was about to leave, having satisfied himself that we had settled down, and we were beginning to resign ourselves to disappointment. Then, finally, there it was. There was the long-hoped for sound – a sound we had never heard before in Thailand. It was the steady roar of heavy bombers, growing louder and nearer with every passing second. Not for a moment did we consider that these might be Japanese planes. We just knew, without a doubt, that they were ours. Minutes later, the proof of this arrived when, as one man, we all leapt off our beds and rushed outside to see a flight of B-17s rushing overhead. The Jap guard stood in the doorway of the hut, looking up at the planes, an expression of disbelief on his face. Here, at last, was something we could hitch our hopes to. We stood outside drinking in this wonderful sight, our shouts drowned out by the noise of the planes' engines. The disappointment which had threatened to sweep over us just minutes earlier had been replaced by feelings of happiness and excitement the like of which we hadn't known since before we had been herded into Changi back in February 1942.

Remembering the rumours of the line being bombed, many of the chaps made their way to the air raid shelters which we had dug some months earlier. These were situated about ten yards to the rear of the huts and were 6 feet deep, 2 feet wide and had been dug in a zig-zag fashion. Most of us just stayed where were, staring at the sky and wondering if the occupants of those planes had any idea of the excitement they had caused in our camp. Suddenly, one of the Japs – a surly individual by the name of Okomoto – stormed across to us with a bamboo pole in one hand and a book in the other. Shouting at the top of his voice, he gave the order for every man to be on parade immediately. Knowing what a nasty piece of work Oko was, we all responded at the double. At the roll-call which followed, one of the chaps was found to be missing – an Aussie called Alec – who quite frequently sneaked out of the camp at night in order to trade with some of the Thais. He was quite a character and was certainly one for taking risks, and this had landed him in hot water more than once. Considering the mood Oko was in, it was only some quick thinking on behalf of one of the other chaps, a Dutch sergeant major, that prevented things from getting very nasty. He said that Alec had been feeling sick at tea time and had mentioned that he was going to ask permission to go to the hospital camp at the next station up the line, so he assumed that was where he was. Although we all knew this was not the case, we also knew that the Jap would be unable to check up on the story until morning, by which time Alec was sure to have returned and would have had time to work on a good excuse for his absence. Oko seemed to accept this explanation for the time being, or perhaps he now had more important things on his mind, as the sight of our aircraft had clearly unnerved him. By this time, the planes were out of sight but from the direction of Bangkok we could hear very heavy rumbling noises and the sky was lit up for miles around. We were all ordered to go to the shelters and to stay there for the rest of the night. The bombing continued for about half an hour and then we heard the planes coming back. As they flew across the camp we counted them. There had been eight the first time they went over, but only seven returned. We hoped the eighth hadn't been shot down and hoped for several return visits.

Not surprisingly, the following morning the only topic of conversation was the B-17s and the bombing we had heard. We hoped that some lucky chance would bring us into contact with some of the Thais who travelled up and down the line, so that we could discover more about the bombing and where it had taken place. The Japanese, too, suddenly became very talkative, asking several of us if we knew what type of planes they had been. They were unsure what to make of it when one of our chaps, who was often ready with a funny quip, said that they had only been light bombers and that the heavy ones were at least twice the size. Over the course of the next couple of months we had many such visits from the RAF and the USAAF, during daylight hours as well as at night. Each raid seemed to be a little nearer until, at last, the target was Tamarkan Bridge, which couldn't have been more than twenty miles from us. This bridge spanned the main river in this part of the country, and had been brought in sections from Java by the Japanese and re-erected, at the cost of quite a few of the lives of our chaps. It was a steel bridge supported by seven pillars of concrete, all of which had been sunk quite a long way down – four on the banks and three in the river itself. The bridge was only used for rail transport and was a very important feature in the Japanese lines of communication, for the only other means of transport across the river was a wooden bridge a short distance away, and this was in no condition to receive the main trains and wagons which were always passing across the river.

As the weeks passed, the raids became increasingly frequent and eventually our station became the target. We soon realised that our air raid shelters gave us little protection, so in an attempt to avoid becoming casualties of our own planes' bombing, we asked the Japs for permission to move the shelters to a safer area. Not surprisingly, our safety was not a priority to them and it was some time before they agreed to this but in the end they relented and we were allowed to search for a spot which was not only concealed from the air but which also had sandy soil. Having found a suitable place, we began digging two shelters large enough to accommodate the twenty-five of us who were left at the camp. Mainly we used these at night, since during the day, if we were working outside when the raid began, it was a case of using whatever cover was afforded by the rocks on the river bank, as we were too far away to get to the shelters. As it was, on several occasions when we were near enough to use them, we found that they were already occupied by Tamils and Chinese. Having made it quite clear to them that these shelters were not for their use, they got to work on digging their own, large enough to hold three or four men. They worked on the assumption that we had picked the safest place in the area and, as a consequence, our formerly well-concealed spot was soon honeycombed with small holes. In an effort to camouflage their digging they pulled up the foliage round about, which had been our natural cover, and placed it over their holes. It was hardly surprising that as a result, our shelters must have been all too obvious from the air and we were often subjected to machine gunning. To make matters worse, the Japanese had dug shelters too, but it was their practice to dig a round hole about 6 feet deep, only large enough to take one man. As the Japanese at the station numbered about sixty, any movement after dark called for great care, and more casualties resulted from these holes than from the air offensive.

Since the raids had first begun, our days and nights had been dominated by the thought that perhaps whatever time we had yet to spend as prisoners could be counted in months, rather than years. The sight of our planes, and having been able to hear the bombing for ourselves, gave us more than just hope, because that was something we had always held onto, even if it had been very difficult at times; it also gave us strength to deal with whatever was still to come, and it changed the way we faced each day. The Japanese had done their very best to grind us down, physically and mentally, and they had succeeded to some extent, but the continual raids lifted our spirits and did more for our constitution than perhaps anything else (even better food!) could have done.

Whenever there was a raid during the day it disrupted the normal order of things and, as a result, our meals became less regular and sometimes very overcooked. This was due to the fact that if an alert was given just before we were due to eat, the cook, naturally wanting to preserve his own skin, tended to leave the rice to take care of itself, with the result that instead of our normal rice meal we would have 'nutty nutty' (the outer crust of the rice) but, given the circumstances, no one minded. It was rare that something could seem more important to us than food, but the sound of our planes was pure music to our ears and worth much more to us than a few measly portions of rice. For those of us in the engine repair shops, the raids also made quite a difference to the work we had to do. We were able to see for ourselves the damage being caused by our planes as a lot of the bomb-scarred engines were sent to this station, the repair work varying from mending broken windows in a cab to fixing a leak in a boiler. The Japanese began to go to great lengths to protect their trains, and detailed a party of our men to build two sheds the shape of Nissen huts over the line, just outside the station, for the purpose of concealing stationary engines. These huts were constructed from bamboo slats and poles, with sheets of corrugated iron for roofs, and the sides were banked up with mud and ballast for protection against blast. As a further measure, whenever there were a number of trains in the station, they were dispersed as quickly as possible into the jungle and covered over with branches to await Japanese-class engines, which were the only ones suitable for the journey further up the line. To any air observer familiar with the line, the stationary train, although covered with branches, must have been quite obvious, for trees didn't grow fast enough between raids to cover up a stretch of line!

As time went on, many animated discussions took place in the workshop between the engineers and the guards as to how they could best protect not only their trains, but also those on board them, whilst those of us who worked there would be listening and trying to work out what they were planning next. We took great comfort in the fact that they were very concerned at the extent of the damage being caused by the raids and realised our planes meant business. After much debate, one of the engineers came up with an idea which would protect the driver and foreman of the train from aerial attack whilst on the move, and this was given the go-ahead. His plan was to build a cement roof on top of the cab and three of us were put to work on the first engine to be treated this way. The idea seemed so far-fetched that, to my mind, it stood little chance of success but, of course, our participation in this or any other scheme the Japanese came up with was not a matter of choice, however much we were loath to do anything which might help them; you did as you were told or you paid the price. First of all, a set of five holes, each half an inch in diameter, was cut in the sides of the cab roof. Then, two sleepers with corresponding holes were placed in position and bolted to the roof of the cab. About eight sacks of mud were then spread over the roof, together with a couple of sacks of gravel. Chicken wire was then fastened to one side of the roof and pulled taut to the other side. On top of this, a very weak mixture of cement was laid. By way of finishing the job off properly, those of us PoWs working on it put our initials in the cement. Whether this acted as a jinx on the engine we shall never know, but a week later it came back, having been machine gunned further up the line. The damage sustained amounted to three holes in the steam dome and one in the main valve, in other words, the two round humps on the engine boiler housing. The driver had reported that the cement roof had cracked in several places, but the bullets and shells had not penetrated the cab via the roof. This news pleased the Japanese, who ordered that other vital parts of the engine were to be treated in a similar manner. However, because so much ballast was used, whenever the engine came under machine-gun attack from the air, the occupants of the cab now tended to be injured by flints from the stones and by ricocheting bullets. The idea was, nevertheless, deemed good enough to warrant more engines being given the same treatment. As each engine was completed, with its wood, stone and cement protection, so other new ideas were put forward. Eventually, one of the engineer officers organised a competition among all the workshops on the line – I believe there were about four of them – for the best protected engine. The winning design passed through our station a few weeks later, the entire engine covered in sleepers 'dogged' together and finished off with a coat of camouflage paint. Ever more ingenious ideas continued to be suggested and one of the later ones we worked on involved us making a jacket of sand-filled bamboo, which was held in place over the body, cab and front door by means of stout wire threaded through each piece of bamboo. The finished article was then covered with fresh jungle grass, twigs and foliage to camouflage it.

We were always very quick to get ourselves away to the river bank whenever we were given warning of a possible raid. The procedure for this was that a board was hung outside the station office, about 2 feet long and 6 inches wide, one side of which had black Japanese lettering on a white background, whilst the other side was plain red. If the white side was showing, it meant that Allied aircraft were somewhere in Thailand, but if the red side was showing, they were in our area. We seldom waited for the latter to appear as we had implicit faith in the marksmanship of Allied airmen, so upon the white board being hoisted we were usually conspicuous by our absence. This disappearing act of ours got us into trouble on a few occasions as the guards had told us that we were to wait for the bombs to fall before making our way to safety. However, we reckoned it was better to risk a beating rather than risk being blown up and, after the first few raids, the guards learned that discretion was the better part of valour and often beat us to the comparative safety of the boulders which bordered the river. We were fortunate in that although four of the Indians were killed by blast and shrapnel during one of the raids, there were no casualties among our chaps. News did reach us, though, of there having been quite a few losses amongst our men further down the line as a result of the bombing. It seemed so very unfair that they should have lost their lives in this way, having managed to survive the deprivations of life on the railway and all that the Japanese had thrown at them, but then that was the tragedy of war.

Chapter Eight

Hope in the Skies

As the end of 1944 approached, so did the prospect of our third Christmas in captivity and, as a result of the Allied bombing and frequent raids, for the first time we had real hope that there would not be a fourth. As with previous years, we resolved to do whatever we could to make it as enjoyable as possible. Once again, we saved up our pay in order to be able to afford a few extras from the canteen for our Christmas meal. However, around this time there was a fifty per cent increase in the price of tobacco and cigarette papers and, as most of us were smokers, our pay no longer stretched as far. (Some of the chaps who didn't smoke took the opportunity of the cigarette paper shortage to make a bit of extra money by buying bibles and prayer books from various sources and selling the pages – ideal for this purpose as they were made of rice paper – at two or three cents a time. Even among those of us who continued to have faith in God, the feeling was that He would understand.) Luckily, we were able to acquire a few bits and pieces of extra food from the local natives who passed by the camp regularly and who had become much more friendly. We suspected this may have been because they had heard good news as to what was happening on the Burma and European fronts, and this friendliness was their way of letting us know. They would never tell us outright of anything they knew in that respect, for fear of Japanese reprisals. This was a very real fear, and certainly the recent bombing up and down the line had made the Japs quite jumpy. We had long been aware that they had a tendency to be unpredictable and to sometimes fly into a rage at the slightest thing but, having been around most of these particular guards for some time, we had, by and large, got to know what to expect of them. Since the raids had started, we had noticed a change in their manner; they were definitely unnerved, and whilst we thought this could only be a good sign in the long term, it made us very wary of them.

As Christmas Day drew nearer, we were still on the lookout for things which would make our Christmas meal one to remember when a train bearing United States Red Cross parcels arrived at our station. Each of these parcels was clearly marked 'Red Cross – one parcel per man', giving us cause to think that we would each be able to enjoy whatever was inside, but we were wrong. Much to our disappointment, the thirty of us who were at the camp at that time were given a total of one and a half parcels between us. (These were the first and last Red Cross parcels I saw during the entire time I was a PoW, and we later discovered that throughout the whole period of our captivity, although quite a lot of such parcels had been provided for us, the Japanese had routinely kept the vast majority of them for themselves.) As most of us in the camp were British, the full parcel was given to us, while the Dutch chaps had the half. It was decided that the fairest way of sharing the contents among the twenty-one of us was to hold a raffle, in which each of us had a chance of winning either a pound tin of jam, a tin of condensed milk, half a dozen sweet coffee cubes, a two-ounce bar of chocolate, a packet of Kraft cheese, six sweet biscuits, a tin of meat paste, a dozen tablets of chewing gum or twenty cigarettes. The raffle was held on Christmas Eve and the eight of us in our hut did very well, between us winning the jam, cheese and coffee – very welcome luxuries!

On Christmas night we sat down to our meal, which had been the subject of much planning and preparation, and enjoyed boiled fish (caught locally with a piece of mosquito netting), boiled rice, sweet potatoes and cheese, followed by 'nutty' with jam, coffee and a cigarette. Our evening's entertainment was supplied by a game of Mah-jong, using a set we had made out of bamboo, the characters having been burnt on. Our stakes were homemade cigarettes, which changed hands many times during the evening, but in the end we decided it didn't really matter who had won and just smoked them. We had discovered some time earlier that Mah-jong was very popular with the Japanese, but that apparently the junior ranks of the Japanese army were not allowed to play it. Not only did the engineers we worked with often spend their spare time either watching or playing it, but there had been several evenings when some of the Japs had commandeered our hut, which was on the outskirts of the camp, so that they could sit and play this game undisturbed. This had been when a high-ranking Jap was visiting the area, the guards' logic being that he and his party of officials wouldn't think of looking for them there. We, of course, had no say in the matter, any more than we did when the guards sometimes came to watch us play, passing comments on the various cards held by each player and so ruining the game. Being as Mah-jong was virtually a national game to them, they seemed unable to resist the temptation to interrupt and advise us on our play. We had learned not to shown any sign of disapproval, as it generally meant a 'buggeroo', a 'jura' and a well-placed back-hander. In order to round off our Christmas meal nicely, and having waited until later in the evening when the guards were less likely to bother us, we all then partook of a bottle of Thai wine which had been acquired by dubious means and which could probably have served the same purpose as petrol! Nevertheless, we all agreed that it was a good way of finishing the evening. We had enjoyed a grand meal and been able to celebrate the occasion despite the Japs, but hoped our next Christmas would be spent on home soil.

Towards the end of 1944, we had heard that the Japanese were planning to build aerodromes on the west coast of Burma, facing the Andaman Sea, and that to this end they proposed to build a road from Wampo to Tavoy, once again using PoWs as their workforce. The fact that the road was to go through the same sort of difficult terrain as the railway and that this was no easy task for men who were anything but physically fit to undertake was of no consequence to the Japanese. Shortly before Christmas, trainloads of men had been brought up the line to the Wampo area to begin work on the road and, after disembarking, were taken across the river in boats to newly erected camps. Since then, we'd been taking load after load of stores from the line over to these camps, including a number of Japanese handcarts. We were told that before work could begin on the road itself, a track wide enough to allow the handcarts to pass through had to be cut through fifteen miles of very dense, hilly jungle. The idea was to make a chain of food and supply dumps along the track with which to maintain the workforce, and we later heard of men having to carry very heavy sacks of rations through the jungle themselves. Because our chaps were continually ferrying stores across to the camps, we were able to find out how things were going, but the news was always bad. By early 1945, scores of men were working on this project, hacking their way through a jungle in which there was scarcely six inches of clear space, while others followed close behind with the stores. A typical load for each man was a sack of rice or vegetables, weighing in excess of eighty pounds. The guards were merciless. The Japanese saw the road as vital to their plans and, as had been the case with the railway, they were determined that it should go through at all costs. Other parties of men had also begun work on the road from the Tavoy end, with the result that those in charge were keen to see who could cover the most ground before both ends met, regardless of the welfare of the men who had to do the work. Before long, the conditions under which the men were forced to work began to take their toll. We heard of several deaths, and illness on a large scale. As a result, men began returning to Wampo in their hundreds. To replace these losses, native labour was conscripted, mostly from Tamils and Chinese. Day by day, from our side of the river, we watched as very sick men were brought over by small boats ready to be taken by rail down to the hospital camps. Our throats went dry at the thought of all those who had been unable to make the journey back and had died and been buried along the way. By now there must have been so many graves along the line, each marked with a bamboo cross; so many men who hadn't made it. The diseases which were causing the most sickness and death were beriberi and malaria. Had there been enough quinine, then perhaps at least some of those lives could have been saved, but what few supplies there were of this were so scarce that there was never enough to go round even a small camp, much less a large one. The medical officers and orderlies were doing all they could, and worked tirelessly on behalf of the men, but often could do very little to help those who had already been in a weakened state due to vitamin deficiency and had little resistance to catching disease. The natives were just as badly off and after a while many began to disappear into the jungle. I say 'disappear' because so many of them were in such a bad state that they went into the jungle in the hope of having a better chance of surviving than if they continued to slave under such awful conditions and with so little food. Death and disease had become horribly routine in our lives and there just seemed no end to it.

Sometimes we wondered what it was that had caused us to be at our comparatively small camp, working as 'maintenance specialists', rather than across the river with these poor chaps or, for that matter, at some of the more northern camps, where we knew conditions were atrocious. Whenever we talked about it, opinion was divided as to whether it was simply down to our good luck or whether some greater power was looking after us. It was very hard to believe that any God who cared could allow so much unnecessary suffering and death to happen, and it seemed to make no sense that some would be spared the worst of it whereas others were not. So there was a strong case for putting it down to luck. But some of the chaps did pray to God for help, just as I did. Mostly I don't think I stopped to think too much about the likelihood of Him listening, but the act of praying was, in itself, a comfort. After all, who else was there to ask for help? For me, having that bit of faith helped, and I think if I'd let go of it, I might also have let go of hope, and without hope I don't think many of us would have lasted very long.

Towards the end of February 1945 we were told that the camp was being closed and we were being sent further down the line to Tamarkan, which is where the bridges that our planes had been targeting were located. By now I had been at Wampo for about eighteen months and had become very familiar with the place, but all that was about to change and, once again, it was the uncertainty about whatever came next that was the hardest part to deal with. As soon as we arrived at Tamarkan we realised things would be very different here. This was a very large camp where we joined four or five thousand other PoWs – English, Australian, American, Dutch and Javanese. At this camp we came under the guard of Korean and Japanese soldiers, rather than engineers, something we were immediately made well aware of as they barked orders at us. Compared to the camp we had just left, everything here was on a much larger scale. We had been living in smaller huts occupied by no more than twenty of us, but those here were about eighty feet long and twenty feet wide, and each of them accommodated a couple of hundred men. Most of the huts leaked whenever it rained and, when the wind blew with any force, they rocked from one side to another. To cap it all, there were no doors, just an open doorway. It seemed strange to be living among so many people again and to be part of a more regimented camp. The Medical Officers, Sergeant Majors and NCOs were the only officers in the camp and were answerable to the Japs for our behaviour and attendance at roll-calls, at which everyone, with the exception of the sick, had to appear. Where we had just come from, roll-calls had been a fairly low-key affair, but not so here, where they were something

107

of a performance. Firstly, the Sergeant Major in charge of each company would stand in front of his men with a board in his hand stating the number of men under his command. The Korean guards would then line up in front of the whole parade and, on the command 'kioski', everyone would come to attention. The Japanese RSM would then come striding onto the parade ground, mount a dais and salute the parade. On the command 'lowri' being given, everyone would stand at ease and the Koreans would make their way to each individual company in order to count the men and check the numbers. When satisfied that all was correct, they would return to their former position. The 'little Napoleon' would then receive a salute from his Koreans, listen to their report and, if everything was in order, salute again and stride off. Performance over. Or at least until later in the day, when we would have to go through it all again.

Within a couple of hours of reaching Tamarkan I ran into Jim, whom I hadn't seen or heard of since the early days of captivity when we'd been in Singapore. He had also only just arrived and as soon as we were able to, we did some catching up and shared the few belongings which had passed the eagle eye of the inspecting guards on our arrival. I was very pleased he had survived, though he looked a little the worse for wear, just as I did, after a couple of years in the jungle. We soon learned that we had been sent to this camp to work on repairing the damage done by Allied bombing, specifically to the two bridges which were of such importance to the Japanese. I had heard about the perils of bridge building from some of the chaps who had worked on bridges elsewhere along the railway; it seemed to be no-one's favourite job, often involving working at height. I'd also talked to some of those who had worked on the viaduct which had been built just up the line from Wampo towards Tarsoe. Here, the sheer rock face rose about two hundred feet above the fast-flowing river and the engineers had decided that since cutting a pathway through the rock was out of the question, the track would go around the side. The result was that some of our men had to hang by a rope harness down the cliff face and make a succession of holes into the rock with hammers and chisels. Numerous poles were then inserted into these holes, and first the sleepers and then the lines were fixed on top of these. This was an incredible task but it was completed in a very short space of time. (Not surprisingly, perhaps, the first engine to use the line was full of PoWs in case any sabotage had been carried out.) At the time we arrived at Tamarkan, the steel bridge had been out of commission for over a week, and supplies had to be brought over on the wooden bridge, which had also sustained some damage. Repairs to both bridges were considered a matter of urgency and working parties were being sent out each day to work on them.

I had very little time in which to take stock of the camp, for the day after we arrived I was sent out on the 'steel bridge party'. I shall long remember my first day there. A party of fifty of us, accompanied by three guards, left the camp at eight in the morning and made our way along the railway track to the bridge, a distance of three miles. On arrival we were allotted our task for the day. Work had already begun on sinking piles into the river bed to take the place of two of the main concrete pillars which had recently been damaged during a raid. I was told that I was to work up on the gantry. In order to reach the gantry, it was a case of walking out on a low-built gangway about fifty yards long and wide enough for two people, and then climbing the scaffolding, which consisted mostly of tree trunks and was in mid-stream. The pile driver was controlled by a wire hawser stretching to the river bank and attached to a specially constructed brake drum which, in turn, was driven by a diesel engine. My job consisted of sitting at the top of the gantry and guiding a quarter of a ton weight onto the piles in order to drive them into the river bed, and each time the weight dropped, the whole gantry would rock from side to side. From my position, forty feet up, it was anything but pleasant, especially as the river was in flood. We had all been very pleased to learn that this bridge had been badly damaged by our planes, and as I viewed the damage from my position on the gantry I felt proud of them for having done such a good job, but at the same time found myself wishing the bridge had been deemed damaged beyond repair.

Work continued on driving these piles into the river bed all day, accompanied by much shouting from the guards, who were only too ready to deliver a whack to anyone deemed not to be working hard enough. Two of the chaps had been given the job of making tea for the party and once *yasmee* was called, brought it over to us. It was tea with a difference here, though not an unpleasant one; as lime trees grew in abundance in this area, the leaves were often picked and boiled with the tea. We had brought the midday meal out with us, which consisted of two four-gallon tins of cooked rice and about two gallons of vegetable stew, which was heated and served with some tea at about 1300 hours, when work was halted and the Japanese went for their own food. Once our meal was finished, everyone took the opportunity of finding a comfortable spot under a tree or alongside a load of piles in the hope of snatching a few minutes' sleep until such time as the guards returned. The engineers' camp was situated about half a mile from the bridge and, as usual, comprised bamboo and attap huts which had been built amongst mango trees. Once we had discovered this, the fruit didn't last long! As soon as the Japs returned, work resumed once more until five o'clock, when another party of men arrived to take over from us, as work on the bridge continued all night. I had been initiated into bridge repairing, and into the pattern of my working day for the time being.

Each day upon our return to camp we had our supper and then attended roll-call at 2000 hours, after which, in the short time before lights out, we were allowed to relax. This being such a large camp, sometimes there would be a concert, and at other times the musicians among us would organize a sing-song. During this time we were also permitted to visit friends in the hospital or, if we so wished, to attend the graves of our chaps in the cemetery, which numbered over twelve hundred. Many of us had lost friends. Looking at all those graves really brought home the sheer scale of the death toll, and that was without all those whose bodies were buried elsewhere along the line. At the Kanburi side of the bridge a memorial had been built to the memory of all who had died whilst building the railway. This was in the form of four stone walls, in the centre of which was an obelisk about 12 feet high. On each wall were a number of marble tablets bearing an inscription in English, Malay, Chinese, Tamil, Thai, Urdu and Japanese. The marble tablets, we later discovered, were originally NAAFI table tops which the Japs had brought from Singapore.

Some of the chaps used this time in the evenings to work on various moneymaking ideas. A few of the Dutch and Javanese made a few dollars by collecting damaged and disused mess tins and cutting them up to make identification discs, complete with name, regiment and religion inscribed on them. Aluminium wire was used to make small chains which fitted round the wrist, and the average cost of disc and chain was one dollar fifty cents. Others who had managed to acquire tobacco from the local traders made cigarettes to sell in the camp, and there were always plenty who were willing to buy. In terms of keeping up morale, having an extra few smokes was, for many of us, almost as important as having enough to eat. Some chaps even traded their ration of rice for a smoke.

After I had been with the day party for a few weeks I was given half a day's holiday and then switched over to night work. This entailed being down at the bridge by 1730 hours, having had supper before leaving camp, and whilst waiting for the Japanese to change over we were allowed to bathe and swim in the river. Work at the bridge went on steadily throughout the night, with the party working in relays, one group resting while the others worked, changing over every two hours. Clothed in nothing but a jap-happy, sitting on top of a gantry, and having to cope with whatever weather came along was not the ideal way of spending a night. After our night's work was over, we would be relieved at 0900 hours and returned to camp. Sometimes there were other jobs to be done but, if not, we were permitted to rest until 1400 hours, when we would then take part in normal camp routine, doing jobs such as cleaning drains or repairing huts. In my case, this daily routine went on until the beginning of May, only interrupted by increasing Allied raids on the bridge and Kanburi. During this time, the wooden bridge was repaired and then once more put out of action, thanks to the combined efforts of Allied aircraft and the monsoon rain having caused the river to swell. Although this latest round of repairs meant a lot of hard work on the part of our chaps, carrying and then replacing heavy timbers, we were all more than happy for our planes to target the bridge again!

Chapter Nine

The Beginning of the End

On 11 May 1945, Jim and I were among a party of forty-five men who were sent further down the line to Kanburi, not to the main camp, where I had spent several months when I first arrived in Thailand, but to a smaller camp a bit further on. This camp was known as Yagati, and it was a Japanese army transport depot. It seemed that once again, for some of us – like me, Jim was also a driver – our engineering knowledge and experience had come to our rescue. We learned that there had apparently been prisoners of war at this place on only one other occasion and we took over their accommodation. This constituted one long hut, at one end of which was a cookhouse, and at the other end, sleeping quarters for the Japanese sergeant major and lance corporal who were in charge of us. Our immediate superior was a Scottish sergeant major known to all as Jock. He warned us to be wary of the Japs, as they were getting increasingly jumpy and unpredictable, due in no small part to the continued bombing of the area. Once again, we had another lot of Japanese to try to weigh up so that we could work out who was the worst amongst them, the one to avoid upsetting at all costs, because every camp seemed to have someone who

115

fitted that bill. It didn't take us long to work out that here this role was filled by a Japanese lance corporal who was known as The Snake and was in direct charge of us. The Jap strength in the camp was about forty men, but working for them, almost in the capacity of slaves, were six Burmese youths who, having voluntarily joined the Japanese army, now appeared to know which side their bread was buttered, as we found them to be very pro-British.

On our first day at this place we were informed that our job was to dig a tank trap around the camp, a distance of three quarters of a mile. Most of the chaps were detailed to this work but Jim and I and a few of the others were instead sent to work in the motor workshop. The work here was quite varied and some days I would be swinging a hammer or using a power drill, others I would be working the forge bellows or doing acetylene welding. It was good to be working with Jim again after those couple of years of having gone our separate ways. In that time I had made other friends, and he had too, but Jim and I had known each other a long while, since the days before we had been reduced to skin and bone, shuffling along in our home-made clogs, scavenging for food whenever the opportunity arose and taking orders from the Japanese. We had been in several sticky situations together, before and during our time as PoWs, and our time at this camp was to prove no different in that respect.

One very rainy day we were taken over to a small underground store in which oxygen cylinders were kept, and told to unload some cylinders from a lorry and put them in the store with the others. Each of these cylinders weighed about 150lb so we decided to carry one between us rather than to each struggle with one on our own. Unfortunately, the

116

guard accompanying us took a very poor view of this, saying, 'one man, one gas tube'. Having had previous experience of this guard in an ugly mood, we didn't hesitate to do as he said and proceeded to carry a cylinder each. Later, we tried to argue that the blame for what followed could hardly be said to have been ours. Having each managed to stagger to the store carrying a cylinder, Jim managed to slide his down very gently against the wall but mine slipped from my grasp, sending a shower of mud over the two of us and also – although he hadn't yet realised it – splashing the guard's face. In retaliation, Jim threw a handful of mud in my direction. It found its target, hitting me squarely in the chest, at which the guard began laughing hysterically. However, his laughter suddenly stopped when, having put his hand up to his face, he realised it had been splattered with mud, at which point he began screaming and raving like a lunatic. We had seen this sort of thing before with the Jap guards – this tendency to be laughing one minute and furious about something the next – and it never failed to be anything but terrifying, because they were seldom without some sort of weapon close to hand. On this occasion, the weapon was a long bamboo pole. Before using it, the guard proceeded to give us a lecture on Japanese etiquette, which apparently decreed that when a Japanese soldier was insulted it was as bad as insulting the Emperor, and that, of course, was the greatest crime known to them. He said that in order to redeem the Japanese honour it was necessary for him to return the insult, at which point he began swinging the pole at each of us in turn. He landed several heavy blows, swinging wildly from one of us to the other, catching us mainly on our arms and chests again and again, and one of my arms was soon completely numb. As he paused to catch

117

his breath and to wipe the mud from his face, Jim and I seized our opportunity to run off while we still could. As soon as we had done so, we realised that it had probably been a mistake.

On our return to the workshop, one of the other chaps told us that he had seen what had happened and reckoned we would be hauled in front of the Camp Commandant, because by running off before the guard had finished with us, we would be seen to have compounded the insult to the Japanese honour. We hoped this wouldn't apply on this occasion, but knew he was absolutely right in what he was saying. During our years of captivity, we had learned that beatings would be over sooner if we kept as still as possible, however difficult that was. Apparently, in the Japanese army, though fatigues were seldom dealt out in punishment, when this did happen the offender would be detailed to receive so many blows to the face or body. Whilst this punishment was being carried out, he was expected to stand to attention without so much as flinching but, should he do so, the punishment would continue. We were expected to behave in a like manner. We nursed our bruises and did our best to carry on with our work as normal for the rest of the morning and at lunch time returned to the hut to join the rest of the chaps. Awaiting our arrival was the Japanese sergeant major who slept at the end of our hut and who we had so far found to be more reasonable than many of the Japanese we had encountered. He called us to one side and told us in fairly good English that we were 'no good' soldiers and had been very foolish, and that owing to the number of Japs in the camp who had witnessed the morning's occurrence, he would have to punish us in order to uphold the prestige of the Japanese army and so that he wouldn't lose face. We knew that to the Japanese, loss of face was a huge issue, and that arguing would simply have made things worse. We gritted our teeth and somehow managed not to move an inch whilst he gave each of us four hard blows on the face with his closed fist, told us we were to be reported to the Japanese Military Police for further punishment (which, for whatever reason and much to our relief, did not happen), and deprived us of half of our rations of rice for the rest of the day.

The withholding of food from men who were already very hungry was a favourite form of punishment of the Japs, and a matter of only a few days later, it was one which was inflicted upon all of us when The Snake, who was never anything other than bad tempered, lost a small piece of scented soap. Such items were a thing of the past to us and he wrongly assumed that one of us had stolen it and made us all parade outside our hut, with instructions to Jock that we were to be kept there until the soap was found. He then proceeded to search our few belongings, but found nothing. After an hour had passed it began to rain and he realised that by keeping us standing there getting a soaking we might become sick and be unable to work the following day. He therefore allowed us to return to our hut but warned us that we would be punished for what we had 'done'. Shortly afterwards, the soap was seen under his bed, where it had obviously dropped from his wash bag. When he was told about this he accused us of stealing it and then replacing it after the search, and promptly gave the order for our rice ration for that day to be halved. The alternative would have been to admit he had made a mistake but, again, that would have involved loss of face, something the Japanese went out of their way to avoid.

At the beginning of July, I was taken out of the workshop and detailed to join the other men who were digging the tank trap. Nearly all of the forty-four of us at the camp were now working either on the tank trap or on air raid shelters. The Japs were also working with us, which made us think that the position in Burma must be getting rather acute from their point of view. During both day and night, Allied air raids were increasing and on several occasions so many bombs fell around us that we thought our camp was being specifically targeted. Night after night, we took with us our rice-sack blankets and huddled down in the shelters, to Japanese shouts of 'yohaw-yohaw', which we decided was some kind of warning that aircraft were approaching. They were clearly becoming very unnerved by all this aerial activity and, at times, seemed more unpredictable than ever. Experience had taught us never to believe anything the Japanese said and always to expect the unexpected of them, but even so, over three years into our captivity, their behaviour still had the capacity to baffle us. As the raids became more and more frequent, there were times when they seemed to be trying to be nice to us! For instance, in mid-July, each time there was a raid on the town, the Japanese adopted the habit of presenting each of us with a coconut doughnut and a cup of coffee at each of the two 'stand easy' periods, 1100 hours and 1500 hours. We didn't know what to make of this, as it was certainly not like them to be so generous. These were the same Japs who had been giving us such pitiful rations and had never shown even the slightest interest in our welfare. We could only assume that our boys were getting near and that the Japs hoped to atone for their treatment of us in the past by softening up a little now. As if a couple of stinking doughnuts and some ersatz coffee were going to make us forget those three odd years! It didn't seem possible that they could really be thinking along those lines, but we could think of no other explanation.

Two or three weeks later, the air raid warning was given at about 1100 hours one morning so, as usual, we made our way to the shelters. Several planes approached and dived low over the town and the camp but, much to our surprise, there were no explosions, just two dull thuds quite close by. We later discovered that these thudding noises had been made by two canisters full of pamphlets and, although the Japanese removed these to their headquarters as soon as the 'all-clear' sounded, half a dozen of the pamphlets came into our hands. They were of two designs: one showed the photographs of all the Allied civil and military leaders, with printing in the Thai language, the other was much smaller and also printed in Thai. Japanese Military Police arrived in the camp the following day and appeared very agitated and were obviously aware that some of these pamphlets had gone astray. They questioned all of us, asking if we had any of them, to which we, of course, replied that we hadn't. They then informed us that if we were lying and were found to have any of them in our possession, the penalty was death. We couldn't help but wonder what it was they were so desperate to keep from us. From that moment on, we thought of little else but those pamphlets and their significance. At the end of each day we would gather together and share our thoughts as we tried to work out what news they might contain about the situation in Europe and Burma. To our minds, given the attitude of the Japs, it surely had to be good news from our point of view, but as none of us were able to translate Thai, we could only guess. Was the war in Europe over, we wondered? And, if it was, were the forces being concentrated on the Far East? One of the chaps managed to ask the Burmese boys in the camp but they would only say, 'England number one. Very soon all finish'. We wondered what they knew that we didn't, but could get no more out of them. Then a group of Thais passed the camp and gave us the thumbs-up sign and shouted to us, 'Churchill velly goot'. We desperately wanted to know what was behind this remark but it finally did seem to confirm that there was some good news out there, even if we didn't know exactly what it was. I had never stopped believing that the Allies would overcome the Japanese, and when we were having a particularly tough time of things, it was that sort of belief that had kept many of us going. Now we had real hope in our hearts.

On the night of 16 August, just after midnight, we were suddenly woken by the guards, hustled out of our beds and told to take all our possessions with us and to squat down in the roadway. To our horror, a machine gun was then mounted fifty yards or so away from us and was pointed in our direction. To be honest, we were in a blue funk. The camp was in the process of being evacuated and as we sat at the roadside, staring at the machine gun, we thought that this was the end for us. We contemplated rushing the machine gun with a view to gaining it for our own use, but Jock said it might be better to wait a short while and see how things developed. We had been sitting there for about an hour when the Japanese Sergeant Major approached us and said, 'very sorry, please go sleep, my instructions from office'. And with that, he smiled and walked away. Very relieved, but very puzzled, we returned to our huts, but sleep was completely out of the question. Why the turn out, we wondered, and why the unheard-of use of the word 'please'? Above all, why the accompanying smile?

After much discussion, we did eventually fall asleep. The following morning, we began to wonder if the events of the previous night had been no more than a dream because, having had our breakfast, we were given our normal work routine. With the exception of three or four men who were detailed to work in the cookhouse or do general cleaning around the camp, the rest of us were sent off to continue work on the tank trap, which was by now nearing completion. A while later, two Japanese officers whom we had not come across before were seen arriving by car at 'stand easy' time. Shortly afterwards, Jock was summoned by the officers and spent about twenty minutes with them. On his return, he wore a smile. When pressed for details he gave a broad grin and said, 'you've waited a long time to hear what I've got to tell you, but it won't hurt to wait a wee while longer'. This felt like cause for real hope, but I think we were all scared of voicing that hope too loudly in case it came to nothing. Mostly we just stared at each other, but I'm sure we were all thinking the same thought, which was along the lines of, 'dare we hope that this hell will soon be over?'

We carried on with work on the tank trap, digging and dirt carrying, until about midday, when we returned to camp for our meal. We had just begun to eat when The Snake appeared on the scene carrying a small blue cloth bag, which he shook so that the contents jingled as he walked about, making us wonder what he was up to now. He stopped at one end of the hut and looked towards us before saying, 'Nippon very good heart – presento', waving the bag around as he spoke. Jock then told us to form into a single line in front of The Snake and, lo and behold, he proceeded to pay us our meagre wage up to date – something which was unheard of in the middle of the month. We asked the Jap if there would be any canteen supplies that afternoon, to which he replied, 'tomorrow, all canteen'. This did nothing to enlighten us, and Jock still held on to his news.

We sat down again to finish our meal, and waited to see if anything else out of the ordinary was going to happen but, when nothing did, we washed our rice bowls and put them away and prepared to get back to our digging. Just as we were about to make our way back to work, the Japanese sergeant major appeared and told us all to pack up our kit as we were leaving. The place was in uproar, everyone trying to work out what was happening but none of us really knowing what to think. We had very little kit to pack and were ready to leave by the time two trucks appeared on the scene. We quickly loaded our belongings into these before the Japanese changed their minds. To make matters even more mysterious, we were told not to worry about taking our kitchen utensils, which we naturally considered to be very valuable assets. Accompanied by two guards, we piled into the trucks and began our journey, unaware of where we were heading and paying close attention to the route being taken. As each turning came into sight we had bets between ourselves as to whether we would be taking it, or going straight on. Eventually, we came to the Pagoda and turned right, which we knew meant that we were headed for Tamuang, which was the largest base camp in the vicinity, surrounded by a bamboo stockade fifteen feet high. Because the surface of the road was so uneven, our progress was very slow, adding to the sense of anticipation we all felt at this sudden turn of events.

Finally, we rounded a bend and came in sight of the camp gates – and what a sight met our eyes. I personally will never experience another moment like that as long as I live. There, against the blue of the Thai sky, fluttered three flags, seeming to beckon us towards that which we had hoped for and dreamed of for so long – freedom. They were the flags of Britain, America and Holland. Walking towards us from the gate with arms outstretched in welcome was an English padre whom we had known for some years. With tears in his eyes, he said, 'God bless you, my boys, you are free.'

This announcement was almost too much for us. We had said that if a moment such as this ever happened, we would cheer out loud. Instead, most of us just sat down in the road and gave way to emotion. Others flung their arms around one another. Free. Such a small word. We had dared to hope that we would live to hear it. Now we had.

After we had composed ourselves to a degree, the padre conducted us into the camp, where there were already two or three thousand PoWs strolling around with an air of ease, smoking proper cigarettes. It didn't seem real. Perhaps it's just a dream, I thought to myself, but I was wrong. This was the real thing. FREEDOM in capital letters! A very well organised reception committee awaited us and in less than half an hour we were given a good hot meal of rice (which, by now, had become a necessity to us), potatoes, noodles and a fried egg, followed by a cup of tea, the latter being remarkable for the addition of milk and sugar. We were shown our billets and, as far as was possible, each man was with his own unit. Jim and I were very pleased to meet up again with some of our regiment and within just a short while we too were strolling around smoking real cigarettes, asking and answering many questions. Outside the camp office was a notice board, on which was posted the latest 'gen', including a daily bulletin of the British news. An enormous crowd was gathered around the board and it was quite half an hour before we were able to read the news for ourselves. It was here that we learned for the first time that the war in Europe had ended in May. The item which interested us most was that which gave details of the Japanese surrender note, which had been signed on 15 August, two days previously. Here, at last, was the reason behind all the commotion in our former camp.

Very few people in the camp slept that night. Instead, we gathered into groups outside the huts discussing the future. Until this day, we hadn't known if we had a future. A few bottles of Thai wine had found their way into the camp and mild celebrations were in progress all round. Strict orders had been given by the senior British official present that no-one was to leave the camp under any circumstances, and that the Japanese guards who were still present at the gates were under orders to turn back any man who attempted to leave. At the time this seemed ridiculous, but we later learned that the order was given for our own benefit. There were plentiful supplies of native alcohol in the town which, as well as being a risk to our already fragile health, would undoubtedly have led to friction arising with the Japanese, had our men been heavily under its influence.

After three days at this camp, Jim and I were detailed to a party leaving for the officers' camp at Kanburi, where we were to be given temporary employment. On arrival we were met by the senior British officer at the camp, a Royal Navy commander. We were shown our sleeping quarters and later met some of the officers from our regiment, among them my own Commanding Officer, under whom I had served for several years before the war. I was pleased to know that he had survived the ordeal, but he had aged considerably. But then, I suppose we all had.

Day by day, increasing numbers of trains arrived from the northern camps, loaded for the most part with very sick men, and the hospital huts in the camp were soon filled to overflowing. Tragically, some men were so sick that they didn't survive their journey to freedom, but whereas before the armistice they would have been buried en route, they were now to be given a decent burial, complete with padre and Union Jack and the Last Post as a farewell. Jim and I were then given jobs as temporary police and had a number of duties. Our chaps were allowed to go into the town, as long as they were decently clothed, between 1500 and 2000 hours, and we were required to patrol the town, accompanied by an officer, with the aim of preventing incidents occurring between any of our chaps and our former captors. Our duties also included preparing the adjoining aerodrome so that it was ready to receive supplies which were to be dropped by the RAF, organising the native hawkers, and preventing unwelcome visitors from entering the camp.

On 23 August a single-engined aircraft came flying very low towards the camp. We later learned that this was a Spitfire, the first one that most of us had ever seen. As it flew overhead, the pilot treated us to some aerobatics – victory rolls – which were also new to us. A few minutes later we heard the sound of heavier planes, and two Dakotas were seen. After circling the aerodrome twice they began dropping containers of supplies by parachute, as the field was too small to accommodate large aircraft. In all, ten containers were dropped, containing Players cigarettes, tins of preserves, tea, coffee, clothing and Red Cross supplies, which were urgently required. A message was also dropped to the effect that, weather permitting, the operation would be repeated the following day. That same afternoon a British officer with a receiving and transmitting radio also arrived by parachute. He was the first person from the outside world we had come into contact with and was besieged with questions. A few hours later a Swiss Red Cross official arrived at the camp and enquired after our general state of health. He seemed a little uneasy whilst surrounded by PoWs and was later heard to remark to the Commander, with many apologies, that the 'stink' amongst the men was overpowering. It was explained to him that this was due to our diet and the way of life we had been compelled to follow. We had lived with the smell of death and disease and out-of-control bodily functions for so long that we scarcely noticed it ourselves any more. Perhaps not surprisingly, from then on all his business was conducted by way of the hastily-erected camp telephone!

On 28 August the Japanese guardroom in the camp was officially handed over with full ceremony. At 1800 hours the camp police – including Jim and me – were warned by the Provost Marshal to be on parade at 1830 hours in full dress. Under the circumstances, this consisted of khaki-drill shirts, slacks, brown boots, leather belt and a brassard bearing the initials 'RP' (Regimental Police). The Provost Marshal arrived on the scene wearing his kilt and tam o'shanter, the remnants of uniform which he had been able to hang onto. He was also wearing, for the first time since 1942, a pistol. Captain B then inspected the parade and reported to the Provost Marshal that the British and Dutch police were all present and correct. We were marched to the Japanese guardroom and came to a halt facing it. The Japanese Commander, a lieutenant, emerged from his bamboo hut and, upon reaching the guardroom, gave the Japanese their instructions. The Guard Commander then sent for his sentries to return from their posts. When all the guards were present they formed up, facing us, with their NCO in charge on their left. The lieutenant then saluted the Provost Marshal and returned slowly to the hut. The guards were brought to attention and we received another salute. They were then dismissed and began to make their way to their quarters, muttering under their breath. Those men of our party already detailed were then ordered to their respective positions of the gate and the guardroom, and the remainder of the police were given instructions to patrol the camp boundary. Never during the entire duration of my captivity had I seen expressions on the faces of Japanese soldiers such as those worn during this changing of the guard. As they were dismissed, one of them, a two-star soldier, began to cry, and the NCO in charge had both tears and hate in his eyes when his salute was ignored. The situation between the Japanese and ourselves had now been completely reversed. They were permitted to leave the camp for two hours each day and, when passing the guardroom, had to bow and salute us for a change. This must have shaken their egos considerably!

Jim and I were then detailed to clear up some of the Japanese quarters and whilst doing this we discovered why our chaps had received so few Red Cross parcels during our captivity. We came across numerous discarded Chesterfield cigarette packs, Spam and preserve tins and various other oddments which had originated in the USA. It was quite obvious where our parcels had gone, and we wondered what other things had been withheld from us. From time to time many of us had witnessed Japanese soldiers smoking American cigarettes and eating tins of corned beef that we suspected had been intended for us, and now we had the proof. Such items would have been much-appreciated luxuries to us, given our diet of rice and more rice but the Japs had clearly decided their need was greater than ours.

The vast majority of the Japanese I came into contact with during those three and a half years showed complete indifference to our welfare, and some were callous and downright cruel. There were, though, a few exceptions among them, some who had a spark of humanity and showed themselves to be pro-British. One of these was a corporal, who was granted protective custody in the camp as a result of his efforts to save the lives of Allied prisoners. He had been in charge of a number of patients at a hospital in Nong Pladuk, to the south of the railway, when the camp had suffered an exceptionally heavy raid and flying debris from a burning truck had caused the hospital huts to catch fire. Many of the patients were bedridden but this Jap had carried them out of the burning huts single-handedly, sustaining severe burns to both his arms and to his head. When our officers heard of this, his name, rank and number were noted so that when peace was declared, mention of his actions could be made to the proper quarters. He actually requested sanctuary in our camp because he felt his pro-British activities made his position unsafe in his own, and was therefore granted protective custody until such time as he could accompany a party of PoWs to Singapore.

On 5 September I left by rail for Bangkok, along with about fifty others. Jim was leaving with a different party, so we said our goodbyes but knew we would see each other again once we were both back on home soil. I had already bade farewell to Bill, who was going back to Aussie, but we vowed we would stay in touch. Once again, we travelled in cattle trucks, but this journey bore no comparison to the previous one; this time we were only ten to a truck, as opposed to thirty, and we were treated like human beings. The journey took two days but seemed longer in the way that journeys do when you're in a hurry to get somewhere, and was quite monotonous, but there was one incident which will long stay in my mind. A train carrying many Japanese wounded was alongside ours for half an hour while our engine was being watered. These men were in a pitiful state, most of them badly wounded and very few of them had dressings on their wounds. The padre who was accompanying us walked over to one of the trucks and asked, in halting Japanese, when they had last had any food. They said that they had a little water with them but had not eaten anything for two days. Upon hearing this, the padre came back over to us and asked if we could forget our differences for just one moment, for they had no food and we had plenty. None of us even needed to think about our answer. We were so relieved at being free men again, we immediately handed over our tins of biscuits, milk and all the fruit we had with us. The Japs were speechless. And I think that in that moment we all realised that after all that had happened to us, we hadn't been robbed of our own capacity for compassion and humanity.

In the early hours of the morning of 7 September, we arrived at Bangkok main station and were met with a terrific downpour of rain. We then had to cross the river on an open ferry, which was a very slow procedure, and by the time we reached the other side, we were soaking wet. Lorries then took us from the jetty to the camp on the racecourse at Bangkok. Allied authorities had only arrived in Bangkok shortly before we had, so arrangements for our reception were not complete, but it was enough for us that we had a straw mattress, two blankets and a hot meal, after which we slept until late the following day. When we awoke we were told by a British officer that we were not to leave the camp as planes were leaving the aerodrome every day bound for Rangoon, with PoWs on board. Despite this, I'm afraid the majority of us were guilty of having a look at Rangoon from the outside of the camp!

On the morning of 11 September, twenty-four of us were taken by car to Bangkok aerodrome where, for the first time for over three years, we spoke to British women, one of whom was Lady Louis Mountbatten in Red Cross uniform. The others wore summer frocks and they certainly made a grand picture to our starved eyes. However, it took us quite twenty minutes before we could pluck up sufficient courage to speak to them! We then partook of immense quantities of tea and cakes in order to prolong their company and conversation whilst we waited for our plane. At 1100 hours we took off in a Dakota, bound for Rangoon. Just over three hours later, after an uneventful journey, we landed on the steel runway at Rangoon where, after having been photographed beside the plane, we were taken under the wing of the Fourteenth Army. One way and another, we were well looked after. The food was wonderful, and rice was provided in the form of dessert if we required it, as most of us still did; the switchover from a main diet of rice to normal food had to be done carefully, much as we wanted to see the last of it. A cinema had been established in a wooden hut, and next to this was a huge NAAFI, where I met up with another of my officers, a major whom I'd served under at Alor Star, before the nightmare of captivity had begun. I was very glad he'd made it, as I had always had the greatest respect for him. Later that day General 'Bill' Slim gave a long talk and welcomed us to the camp. At the end of the day, housed very comfortably in tents, complete with camp beds, sheets and pillows, we slept like tops.

The remainder of our time in Rangoon was spent sightseeing, but this didn't amount to much as the bomb damage was considerable. Eventually, on 15 September, we boarded the SS *Corfu* and at 0700 hours began our journey home. That same afternoon I was admitted to the ship's hospital after what I'd thought was just a chill turned out to be malaria, coupled with dysentery. When we arrived at Colombo three days later, I was taken ashore on a stretcher and transferred to the 35th British General Hospital (BGH) at Mount Lavinia, where I remained until 1 October. I was then moved from the hospital to the Hill Station convalescent camp at Diyatalawa, where other ex-PoWs had also been sent whilst I was in Colombo, so I found myself among friends.

The name 'Diyatalawa' means 'happy valley', and the place was very aptly named in my case. Just a few weeks earlier, along with several other chaps, I had been staring at the wrong end of a machine gun and wondering if my time was up, and now, in the tranquil surroundings of the convalescent camp, life had begun to look very good indeed. I spent the next six weeks there, the climate and conditions gradually helping me to regain my health. During this time, various outings and picnics were laid on for us, and these did much to help bridge the gap between PoW and civilian life. It was at one of these picnics that I met Joan, a VAD from the Naval Hospital, who is now my wife.

On 11 November 1945, after saying goodbye to the many people who had been so good to us – not forgetting Rajah, the Indian boy who used to bring us early morning tea – a party of us returned by train to Colombo. We spent the night in Echelon Barracks, and at 1000 hours the following day we went aboard the SS *Strathnaver*. Amid the hooters and cheers from the other ships in the harbour, we passed through the boom at 1500 hours. At this time, although I was not aware of it until reaching Southampton, Joan had received the news that she, along with four other nurses, was to sail for home on 17 November. Our ships were separated by a matter of just a few days throughout the whole journey.

Joan and I met once more in mid-December, were married a month later, and now our most treasured possession is our two-week-old daughter who, but for faith, hope and (mostly) rice, would certainly not be smiling at us now.

Tony Cox
(May 1947)

Postscript

[For the many thousands of British and Allied servicemen who returned home after three and a half years of captivity by the Japanese, the war was far from over. They had their freedom, but the conditions to which they had been subjected during those years left them with a legacy of physical and psychological problems. It was with this in mind that in 1990, shortly before he died, Dad began to work on a brief postscript to his story.]

When I first began to tell this story it was 1946. Now, nearly forty-five years later, I can look back and know that for me, and for many others like me, the war did not end in August 1945. Parts of it remained to be coped with and still do, to this day. Much has been written over the years about the terrible conditions thousands of us were forced to endure as prisoners of the Japanese. What none of us were aware of back then, as we tried to put the past behind us, was that as a result of those conditions our health had been irreparably damaged. Like thousands of others, as a consequence of the totally inadequate diet provided by our Japanese captors for three and a half years, I suffered from extreme vitamin deficiency. A diet consisting of poor quality rice and very little else gave us no vitamins A, B, D, E or K. We were aware at the time that a number of the diseases we suffered from were attributable to vitamin deficiency. What we hadn't realised then, however, was that this would have severe implications for our long-term health. Many of us, myself included, had over the years acquired deficiency diseases such as beriberi, and came home with failing eyesight, anaemia, skin ailments and various other problems which, although we weren't aware at the time, would need treatment at clinics and hospitals for years to come. Certainly in my case, this has meant far too many long periods spent in hospital being treated for various problems when I should have been enjoying family life. For instance, it was during my sixth or seventh long spell in Queen Mary's Hospital, Roehampton, that I learned of our second child being born in another hospital over thirty miles away. My wife and I did, however, consider ourselves very lucky to have our children because another less obvious consequence of vitamin deficiency, and one which we only became aware of as time passed, was the effect on fertility. We had decided to start a family as soon as possible after we were married, but it was seventeen months before our first child was born, and a further five and a half years before we were blessed with a second. By this time we knew of many people who had not been as fortunate, who wouldn't go on to know the joy of not only children but, in time, grandchildren – in our case, five of them.

In 1950, thanks to my wife's persistent letter writing, I was awarded a pension – not a large one, but at least the government recognised that my disabilities were brought about whilst I was serving in HM Forces. Having to spend months at a time in hospital rather than working meant that there was very little money to go around so any extra was very welcome. To make matters worse, nerve damage to my spine meant that I was somewhat limited in the type of work I was able to undertake. None of this has stopped me from having a good life. Indeed, there has been much happiness, but at times the going has been very tough and I wouldn't have got through those times without my dear wife's love and support.

It is now forty-five years since we left those camps, but many former prisoners of war still carry not only the physical scars from those years of captivity, but also the kind of scars which cannot be seen. Some have felt unable to talk about what they experienced, ever, to anyone. Back in 1945, when we met people from what we then thought of as the outside world for the first time in three and a half years, I know I wasn't the only one who felt that perhaps the only people who could really understand what those years had been like were those of us who had been there. Amongst ourselves there was no need to try to explain anything, but with other people it was hard to find the words to try to describe the awful things we had seen or the things we had sometimes had to do in order to survive. It had been our own hell and sharing it with others was difficult.

So this is my story, which may, perhaps, help someone else to put life into perspective and will, I hope, help others to remember those who were not as fortunate as I was – those who did not come home. Oh, and one last thing ... I still like rice.

Tony Cox (1990)

Dad was still tinkering around with the wording of this postscript shortly before he was admitted to hospital for the last time, so it is possible that, had he been able to, he would have added more. Therefore, I feel that it falls to me to do so on his behalf, whilst also filling in a few gaps and adding something from my own perspective.

Dad arrived back in England at the end of 1945, having heard nothing from his family for the duration of his time as a PoW, and was therefore relieved to discover that his mother, brothers and sister had all survived the war. They had all settled in or around London, as had Mum's family, and within a few months, Mum and Dad settled down to married life in the same area. Their first home was a Nissen hut, which was, for many at that time, the answer to the shortage of post-war housing due to the heavy bombing there had been around London. Within a few months, however, and with some help from Mum's family, they managed to scrape enough money together for somewhere more substantial – somewhere they could really call home as they focused their thoughts upon building a future together, raising a family and putting the horror of the war years firmly behind them. However, this proved difficult, as by the time I was born, in the early 1950s, it had become clear that dad's health had suffered long term damage as a result of his years as a PoW.

As I grew up, although it was something I became aware of only gradually over time, the consequences of Dad's years of captivity were ever-present in our lives. I remember as a child being taken to visit Dad in hospital, where he spent weeks at a time being treated for various ailments. I was too young at the time to have any inkling that these hospital stays were a consequence of the years he had spent in captivity before I was born and the awful conditions to which he had been subjected by the Japanese. Not long after Dad and his fellow ex-PoWs had been repatriated it was recognised that a large number of them were seeking help for medical conditions which appeared to be linked to diseases they had acquired whilst in captivity, and from various neurological disorders associated with these. Some of these were tropical diseases such as malaria and dysentery; others were nutritional deficiency diseases such as beriberi and pellagra. In response to this, a specialist unit was established at Queen Mary's Hospital, Roehampton, in south-west London to treat them. Within a few months of coming home, Dad was admitted for the first of many stays there, and visiting him in this hospital became a part of my childhood, entailing a journey of some thirty miles involving a train and at least two buses. He was often in Roehampton for six to eight weeks at a time and we would travel to see him at weekends or as often as shortage of money allowed. I had no idea what Dad was being treated for at the time but now know that some of his stays in hospital related to him having been left with nerve damage to his spine, and others to him being treated for some sort of disorder with his bladder, as well as recurrent bouts of malaria. The only ailment of Dad's of which I was well aware as a child was that of a skin condition, which caused him great discomfort when it flared up in periods of hot weather. He would regularly soak his hands and lower arms in a purple solution of permanganate of potash – a ritual which, as a young child, I found fascinating – and Mum would then apply bandages to his arms and he would cover his hands with white cotton gloves. Though I don't remember exactly what I was told in relation to this condition, it was something to the effect of it having been caused by his time in the Far East.

139

I remained largely unaware of the enormity of what Dad and others had been exposed to as prisoners of war for many years because I was given a very sanitised account of events and, even then, it was no more than a gentle drip-feeding of information, usually in response to my questions, and with great emphasis on the issue of how hungry everyone had been. Only much later did I realise that I had been given a somewhat diluted version of reality, devoid of many of the more horrific aspects of those years of captivity and illustrated with relatively light-hearted anecdotes concerning the various ways in which Dad and his pals had managed to acquire extra food. It was something he chose to speak of only occasionally and usually in an understated way, and I therefore grew up with very little real appreciation of what Dad had been through. By contrast, he and Mum spoke often and with great fondness of the brief time they had spent together in what was then Ceylon, where they had first met – the places they had visited, the friends they had made, the joy of sharing together the simple pleasures of life as the world emerged from the shadow of war.

The only real clue in those early years to the fact that his time in captivity had left its mark on him psychologically lay in Dad's attitude towards food, which left several childhood memories seared into my mind. No doubt in the post-war years of austerity ours wasn't the only household in which there was an abhorrence of the idea of wasting food. However, I doubt many parents of young children took things to the same extreme as mine. We were simply not allowed to leave food on our plates. Ever. Disliking a particular kind of food cut no ice at all; we were told that it was good for us, that it was full of vitamins and that we had to eat it. Consequently, if I refused to eat the Brussels sprouts I so loathed at lunch time, they would be served up again at tea time. If I still refused to eat them, they would reappear the following morning for breakfast, and so on. I do remember once rebelling against this practice by throwing a plate of food on the floor and then receiving what was in those days termed 'a good hiding'. However, in time I grew to learn that I was unlikely to win this battle over food and generally ate whatever was put in front of me, however unpalatable it seemed. My parents were in total agreement on this issue, Mum having seen at first hand the dreadful, malnourished state the men had been in when they were recovered from the camps. She told me many years later that when Dad had been brought into the hospital at Colombo he weighed no more than seven and a half stone (he was over six feet tall), his skin a yellowish-grey colour with bones poking through.

Similarly, as a child I clearly remember that Dad would often stress the importance of vitamins, reinforcing the point by regularly drinking the water in which vegetables had just been cooked. He would savour this as a treat, often urging me to try some though, thankfully, not insisting in this case. I remember being told that my teeth would fall out if I didn't have enough vitamins; Dad had lost most of his whilst a PoW and those which remained had had to be removed due to gum disease, which he had acquired as a result of vitamin deficiency. An equally vivid memory is more pleasant: although like many men of that era, Dad didn't do a great deal of cooking, there was one dish which he took great pride in cooking – rice pudding. He would remove the dish from the oven, the top browned to perfection, and place it on the table before us with a look of great satisfaction. Although it would have been entirely understandable had he never wished to eat rice again, years later he told me that he had made a point of learning to cook this dish properly as a way of not letting the Japanese win, and that, furthermore, he had a lot to be grateful to rice for, as it had helped to save his life.

Dad's preoccupation with food wastage and vitamins aside, there are other things which suggest that his perspective on life was influenced by the years of captivity. His abhorrence of waste was not confined to food, and he was reluctant to throw anything away lest it be needed at some point in the future. The ingenuity which had been harnessed in the camps and put to such good use in the battle to survive presumably inspired in him a 'make do and mend' philosophy. Whilst this had undoubtedly proved useful in their early years when there was very little money to go around, it continued beyond the point where there was any real financial need and would, on occasion drive Mum to distraction. Similarly, having lived through the ordeal of captivity and having had to deal with numerous associated problems as a result, Dad was intolerant of those who complained about what, in his view, were trivial matters, and irritated by those who took their good health for granted. However, despite the impact of those years on both his mind and body, whatever Dad's feelings towards his captors, he said he felt no bitterness towards the generation of Japanese who came after them. Nevertheless, it was noticeable that he and Mum went out of their way to avoid buying goods made in Japan.

It seems inconceivable that any of those who returned from three and a half long years in the camps were not changed irrevocably by their experiences as prisoners of war of the Japanese. Many, like Dad, will have carried physical reminders which will have impacted on their quality of life, from amputated limbs to debilitating diseases. More, perhaps, will have suffered psychological damage as a consequence of their prolonged exposure to so much brutality, death and disease and the fact that it occurred in an age which recognised neither post-traumatic stress disorder nor the concept of counselling as an appropriate response to those who had been traumatised. They were, in the main, left to deal on their own with the imprint left on their minds by the cumulative effect of events once witnessed, never forgotten, of friends dying needlessly for want of basic medical supplies and of the callous indifference to their fate shown by their captors. It is little wonder, therefore, that so many chose to bury the past rather than ever speak of it.

It was a psychiatrist at Roehampton who advised Dad that talking about what he had been through might help rid him of the nightmares that were stopping him from getting on with his life. It was Dad's good fortune to have encountered such a (for the time) forward-thinking clinician because whilst 'talking things out' might not have worked for everyone, he felt that for him it had proved the answer. That is not to say that Dad's experiences did not leave their mark on his mind, but perhaps only he knew just how much. By the time I was born, Dad had had over seven years to fight his demons and to learn how to live with his experiences as a prisoner of war and it may be that there were some aspects of this which he kept to himself. Mum mentioned that in their early years together Dad had found it difficult to come to terms with the various ways in which the years of captivity had affected him physically, and that on occasion he became quite depressed and frustrated by his limitations, though theirs was evidently a happy marriage. As a child I was quite oblivious to any personal battles Dad may have been struggling with and so, by and large, for me it was a childhood of happy memories, one in which despite there having been little money to go around, there was no shortage of love or laughter.

Dad was just one of many former Far East prisoners of war whose lives continued to be affected by their years of captivity long after they had left the camps. In addition to the specialist unit which had been opened for them at Roehampton shortly after their repatriation, a similar unit was also established in Liverpool at around the same time. Dad continued to be treated at Roehampton until the late 1960s, when that unit closed, but recurring problems with his back, with his skin and with what he euphemistically referred to as his 'waterworks' dogged him periodically throughout his life, causing him to be hospitalised elsewhere a number of times in the 1970s and 1980s. Others, too, continued to need treatment for a variety of complaints which were found to be linked to the diseases they had contracted whilst held captive, and the Liverpool unit remained open to treat them, with the Liverpool School of Tropical Medicine having since conducted research into the long-term health effects of Far East imprisonment which has revealed the true extent of the legacy borne by many as a result of those three and a half years of captivity.

In Dad's case, so much time spent in hospital had severe implications for his working life. Shortly after he and Mum settled down to married life he had joined the Fire Service. However, within months the work proved to be beyond him physically, as the lifting it entailed aggravated the problems with his back and saw him admitted to hospital several times. After quite a long period of time out of work, he managed to secure a job with the GPO, who proved to be quite sympathetic employers as far as his time off for sickness was concerned, and he stayed with them for over twenty years, until a couple of heart attacks in his late fifties compounded his other health problems and he was advised to retire on medical grounds.

Dad remained in contact with some of those with whom he had spent time in various PoW camps for many years, and also attended several FEPOW reunions in London until the 1970s, after which he and Mum moved away from the area. No doubt he found the shared understanding which existed among his fellow ex-PoWs a source of comfort as he endeavoured to come to terms with his experiences, and the bond between them gave rise to some deep friendships. Having been such close friends with Jim before and during the war, he remained so for several years but then lost touch with him in the late 1970s. However, two other friendships forged in captivity lasted a lifetime. Although Bill, whom he had met whilst they were at Wampo, went back to Australia at the end of the war, he and Dad wrote frequently, swapping photos and family news for over forty years until Bill's death in the 1980s. Even then, Bill's daughter continued this correspondence for the rest of Dad's life, much to his delight. The other friendship which endured was with one of Dad's former commanding officers, a major in the Air Liaison Intelligence Section in Malaya, to which Dad and his friend Jim had been temporarily posted a few months before the Japanese invasion. Following the fall of Singapore and a brief period at Changi, Dad and his former CO, Gerry, did not see each other again until 1945, when they met in Rangoon on their way back home. However, once back in England, they corresponded regularly over the years and even met up now and then. Dad's friendship with both Jim and Bill was easy enough to understand since they were of the same rank and also the same age. Dad's friendship with Gerry seemed less easy to understand, since not only was he a major to Dad's private, but he was at least twenty years older. I was aware that Dad had been his driver when they were based at Alor Star in Malaya, and Dad always spoke of him with great respect, but this did not explain why theirs was such a close friendship. I remember asking Dad about this many years ago and he said something along the lines of there having been times during the war when rank had little meaning, and that sometimes other things, such as the need to survive, simply transcended it. They remained in contact until Gerry's death in the 1980s, after which his daughter also continued to write to Dad. It was from her that I learned, after Dad's death, what had been at the heart of their friendship. It transpired that Gerry credited Dad with having saved his life when they had come under heavy fire from the Japanese in Malaya – something which Dad had never mentioned, though presumably Mum knew about it. Dad never spoke in any detail about his time in Malaya which, by all accounts, must have been particularly tough as over two thirds of his battalion were killed. Since it seems likely that some of those lost to battle were friends, perhaps there were some parts of his war which were simply too painful to talk about and remained consigned to the past.

Dad loved the Army and was proud to have served his country but he said that he felt let down by the way he and his fellow former PoWs had been treated. Specifically, he felt let down by a system which required him to attend a medical every year in order to establish whether or not he was still deserving of the small invalidity pension he had been awarded in 1950 in recognition of the fact that his disabilities had been incurred whilst a serving soldier. He

146

had been told by several different doctors that the damage to his spine was permanent, and he walked with a limp, yet still he was required to attend annual medical checks, something which he found rather farcical and which made him quite angry. He felt similarly about the payment of around £75 which he and all British former PoWs had been awarded in the early 1950s, which he considered a paltry sum for those who had served king and country with pride, many of whom had almost died in the process. Sadly, Dad did not live long enough to benefit from the one-off *ex gratia* payment of £10,000 which the government somewhat belatedly saw fit to award all surviving British PoWs in 2000 in recognition of their suffering.

Dad would be the first to say that there was nothing heroic in his having survived an experience which claimed the lives of so many. What he went through, thousands of others also went through, and he acknowledged that whilst his experience of those years of captivity had left its scars upon him both physically and mentally, he had suffered no more than anyone else and less than many others; crucially, he had come home, when so many others had not. He never forgot those whose lives ended beside a railway track in the Far East, well aware that his life could have been snatched away by disease just as easily as many of theirs had been. Now, nearly seventy years after the Japanese surrender and the liberation of the thousands who were held captive, relatively few former FEPOWs are still alive. Many, like Dad, will be remembered first and foremost as much loved family members. However, it is surely up to future generations to perpetuate their memory as former prisoners of war and to not allow the world to forget how much they sacrificed in the service of their country.

***

Index